# Feet to the Street

## Becoming an Instrument of Revival

### Rose Rizzi

AMBASSADOR!
PO. BOX 9843
KANSAS CITY, MO. 64134
(816)-965-0509

First printing October 1999
Printed in United States of America

**Library of Congress Catalog Card Number: 99-12045**
**Andrews, Rose Rizzi**
**Feet To The Street/Rose Rizzi Andrews**
**ISBN 0-9675552-0-5**




**Published by AMBASSADORS PRESS**
**Kansas City, Missouri**
**Printed in the U.S.A**
**Cover design by Christopher Rowney**



**For further information, contact AMBASSADORS PRESS,**
**PO Box 9843, Kansas City, Missouri 64134**

# Recommendations for
# *"Feet to the Street"*

**F**eet to the Street is a powerful picture of prophetic evangelism. It challenges the Body of Christ to shake out of their complacency and see the people that pass by us every day as those that Jesus gave His life to save. You will laugh, be encouraged, and find a new love for the Lord as you read its pages.

*Cindy Jacobs*
*Cofounder of Generals of Intercession*

**T**his book burns with the flame of passion for Jesus and illustrates the kind of faith and obedience that makes possible a contagious witness for Him.

*J. Wesley Adams*
*Coauthor and editor of the Full Life Study Bible*

**R**ose Andrews reveals God's love and wonder working power in very practical ways. Her message challenges us to focus on what God's purposes are for His people. We discover that God is still in the business of blessing us not because of who we are, but because of who He is. When I consider what God has done in Rose's life and ministry my heart is encouraged and my faith is stretched. She has been a blessing to many as she has touched them with her life in Christ. As you read this account of God's faithfulness, you will be greatly encouraged to believe Him to be faithful to you. I find God to be very real and personal through Rose's experiences which makes me delighted to endorse this story of a life being forward for His glory.

*Don Richter*
*Director of Harvest Preparation International Ministries*
*Sarasota, FL*

**R**osey keeps the focus on Jesus and her feet on solid biblical ground. Dramatic things happen but she is never the hero; she simply obeys Jesus and gives Him all kinds of prayers to answer. I'm sure you're going to find practical wisdom that will empower you to cover your community with life-giving prayer. She is a virtual one-woman school of courage in prayer. Read this book!

*Steve Hawthorne*
*WayMakers/PrayerWalk USA*
*Austin, Texas*

# Dedication

To my mom and dad whose arms are always stretched out and whose hearts are as big as the outdoors. They have worked through and walked through so many seasons with me so that I have the liberty to live out my destiny.

And to my husband Bill whose manhood shines strong and confident giving me the freedom to be me.

*"For Zion's sake, I will not be silent,...."*

*Isaiah 62:1*

# Contents

Acknowledgments ~~~~~~~~~~~~~~ ix

Introduction ~~~~~~~~~~~~~~~~ 1

A Voice Like A Trumpet ~~~~~~~~~~ 5

A Fish Chapel ~~~~~~~~~~~~~ 9
*(Faith, two ice chests and $50)*

Back Home ~~~~~~~~~~~~~~~~ 25
*(Apprenticed by God in my hometown)*

Who is Living In You? ~~~~~~~~~~ 39

Bus 23 ~~~~~~~~~~~~~~~~~~ 51
*(God shows up at the bus garage)*

Giessin Germany ~~~~~~~~~~~~ 61
*(The greatest gift is love)*

American Soil ~~~~~~~~~~~~~~ 79

Taking the Bride To The City ~~~~~~ 87

Authority vs Permission ~~~~~~~~ 99

OH NO! Transition Again ~~~~~~~~ 107

Next Exit Grandview ~~~~~~~~~~ 117

Your Feet Play A Significant Part ~~~~~ 129

Epilogue: ~~~~~~~~~~~~~~~~ 137

Appendix ~~~~~~~~~~~~~~~~ 139

# Acknowledgments

I don't know where I'd be without Jesus Christ. I wouldn't even have penned this book. His Spirit gave me the grace and guidance every step of the way. I want to give Him all the Glory that's due to His Name for what He has done in and through my life, so first and foremost I say, "Thank you Jesus."

Having a husband like mine is a rare thing. Bill, you encourage me to be all I can be for Jesus. You allow me the freedom to give my life away without reservation. You are my best friend and lover for life. I want to express my deep appreciation to you Bill, for sacrificing hours of our time together and allowing me time to write this book. You are a hidden treasure.

There were several of my friends that sacrificed time reading the manuscript, bringing well-needed corrections and letting me bounce ideas off them whenever I wanted to. They gave of themselves without seeking reward, recognition or monetary exchange. This book was made possible through their prayer support, work and encouragement. I am immensely grateful for your assistance and blessed to know your help to me was an extension of your true friendship towards me. Eva Mahan, Bruce Keller, Jocelyn Smith, Rod Girgan, Dale Hensley, Molly Geary, Carol Hoffmeier, Faye Dunbaugh, Leslie Douglas, D Weber and Kathleen Palmer and the incredible assistance from David and Deborah from the UMKC Writers Lab; I pray the Lord richly blesses each and every one of you with all of your heart's desires. Thank you so much for your help and support.

And certainly my editing staff: Jackie McGirvin, Dan Nichols, Leslie Douglas, and Designer/Typesetter Christopher Rowney — Thank you.

With a Thankful Heart,
Rose Andrews

# Introduction

The writing of a book has been on my heart for a long time. It has been a tremendous undertaking beyond anything that I ever anticipated. Nevertheless, it has been exciting contacting friends, reminiscing about the ways God has both met us in the past and is still meeting us today, right in the middle of our everyday lives.

*"Feet to the Street"* is a journey through my history as Jesus molds me into a vessel that can be used to prepare the way for Him to encounter others in practical, everyday circumstances.

The Holy Spirit draws me into a challenging lifestyle of intercession and devotion to Jesus that opens doors in my heart to the needs of those in my surroundings that otherwise would have remained shut. Beyond comprehension, I'm moved to pray wherever I am for release of the Holy Spirit upon other's hearts. Much to my surprise the laundromats and local grocery stores become the hot spots as the Lord puts His hand on the simplest conversations with the lost, prodigals, Christians and even unchurched believers.

In *Feet to the Street,* I have found the grace from Him to share my understanding and experiences in the same way that He brought them to me, simple and clear. That's the way the "Good News" should be. If we walk in the simplicity of devotion to Christ, we will find that reaching out to our society with the power of the kingdom will be a natural outflow of that devotion. Just as it is written in the Word, if we abide in Him, we will bear much fruit.

The heart of the Father has not changed. His house shall be called a house of prayer for all nations. This house is a living temple not made with hands. It is our very living beings. We are the living stones of His temple. Because we are living stones, we can pray wherever we are. On-site prayer literally changed the normal circumstances at my workplace before my very eyes.

1

My earnest desire is that my everyday experiences will encourage ordinary Christians to walk with a conscious awareness that the presence of God allows Him the opportunity to use them to bring the kingdom of God into their own surroundings. I believe God is raising up equippers throughout the body of Christ who will model this simplicity and mobilize the local church to do the work of Jesus Christ in ordinary lives.

The need is arising for believers to see themselves commissioned to full time service in our everyday settings. Recently the Lord gave me a word picture to help explain this to the body of Christ. I call it "Adopt Your Street." This is where individuals commit to pray and watch over their own streets, like policemen on the beat, continually inviting God to permeate their neighborhoods.

Our love for Jesus cannot be hidden under a bushel basket. He is willing to use us prophetically, pastorally, and evangelistically to allow our lives to train others right in our own environment. We don't have to be hired staff in a church or wait until we acquire the title of apostle, prophet, pastor, teacher or evangelist. Even newly saved believers can be encouraged to pray for the needs of those around them and see the greatness of God manifested in answered prayer. It's time to rise up and be full time Christians and utilize every opportunity that comes our way to shine the light of Jesus through on-site prayer.

I began with baby steps trusting God to love others through me even in my own brokenness. I discovered that merely making myself available to be used by the Holy Spirit is a big key to seeing Him move. The mistakes made along the way have all been turned into instruments of wisdom by Jesus to help me remember I am a weak human being without Him. They have taught me to trust in His strength, the power of His might, and the futility of leaning on my own understanding. He was and is still faithful to teach me His wise ways and direct me in His righteous paths.

As the final hour in God's redemptive plan begins to tick away, I believe a cry is going forth from the heart of God for His people to kick out the props, the labels and the programs. God is seeking wholehearted lovers and sincere friends that will invite Him into every part of our lives. Just having coffee with your boss or offering a deed of kindness to your neighbor, I am amazed how frequently Jesus turns regular conversations completely around for His glory. The Holy Spirit through prayer initiates these encounters. Prayer is the most amazing weapon of warfare given to us as joint heirs in Christ. If we persist in prayer, God will always make a way where there is no way, no matter what setting we are in.

When I thought about writing this book, I went to the local bookstore to inquire how many books are on the shelves that encourage the importance of on-site prayer. The few I could locate on this subject were *"Prayerwalking"* by Steve Hawthorn and Graham Kendrick, *"That None Should Perish"* by Ed Silvoso and *"Primary Purpose"* by Ted Haggard.

Sadly, only a few mentioned the significance of on-site prayer. There is nothing like praying for a face that's right in front of you with need written all over it, or sensing the oppression while you're walking down a street and asking God to send forth His light. What better way to fuel the flames of intercession than to ask your neighbors for prayer requests?

The body of Christ in the Western world is in desperate need for a revival in our approach to reaching out. God passionately seeks to touch those outside the walls of our church with His glorious gospel. Prayer Walk USA, Harvest Evangelism, March for Jesus, Global Harvest Ministries, Generals of Intercession and others are equipping us to reach beyond the four walls of our churches into desperately needy communities who might never walk into our buildings.

May God pour out His grace on His Bride and cause us to return to the simplicity of loving Him with all of our beings as Mike Bickle eloquently encourages the body of Christ, so that we in turn pour out His love freely to our neighbors.

My hope is that *Feet to the Street* will help Christians take simple steps forward in their own lives to touch those in their community. I am confident that the love of God for the lost and the joy of reaping the harvest is contagious.

Are you ready to take your feet to the street?

# Chapter 1

# *A Voice Like A Trumpet*

The beach, the sun, and the water were like paradise. What a blessing to leave New York for the winter and be able to take my job with me to Florida. I was the lead singer in a traveling show band. I worked with some of the best guys around. They treated me like royalty and made me feel very special. Our group never lacked work; in fact we were in demand.

I started singing in a band at 17 and this lifestyle had me constantly on the move. My Christian growth was stunted because I couldn't attend the same church regularly. When I did attend somewhere, I just didn't feel like I fit.

Being around church folk seemed uncomfortable, but I kept seeking the Lord. On the road, I watched Christian television. No matter where I went, I kept running into Christians. God was on the move beneath the surface where human eyes could not see.

Each time we moved to another booking location, I scoped the area for two things: a health food store and a church. I learned the hard way about the importance of taking care of my physical body and there was a great desire in me for more of Jesus.

Everything that happened was tenderizing my heart and drawing me deeply into worship. I ran into remarkable Christian people. Our conversations about the Bible were stimulating and satisfying. One day I met three Christians who were witnessing on the beach. I told them I was a nightclub singer and they even came to see me perform. These events confirmed for me that I needed to belong to a church.

I was sure that this particular week these three Christians had been praying for me. The air was so clear and fresh I felt the Holy Spirit throughout that entire week.

All these unusual occurrences built up to an astonishing thing. While jogging one day my heart was suddenly overwhelmed with the goodness of God. I believed with all my heart that He knew right where I was because He had been sending people my way to share with me. Jesus was inviting me into a closer relationship with Him. As I ran, I thanked God for all the wonderful blessings of that day. Then I said, "Lord, You are so good and so wise, I want all You have for me. It doesn't matter what I have to do." I guess that was what the Lord was waiting to hear because suddenly, a white mist engulfed me. I could feel a thick and tangible presence of God (I know now that this was the glory of God). I spoke in a breath-taking new language! It flooded out so eloquently, just like a pent-up river that had broken through a dam. It was as if I had spoken in tongues all my life. I couldn't feel the ground under my feet. It felt as though I was flying. I wept. What a fool I was not to have asked for this gift before! How could I have been so stubborn and arrogant when people spoke to me about it?

When I was about 17 I heard people singing in tongues. I didn't embrace it as being from God, nor did I desire it.

My heart overflowed with repentance as I asked Jesus to forgive me. He was meeting me in spite of myself. All I wanted to do was express my gratitude to Him for His sweet mercy. Even in my unbelief, He waited for the moment when I would ask for more of Him.

I know now that this was all the Holy Spirit's doing. He inspired me to ask for all God had for me. I wondered what would have happened if those Christians hadn't met me on the beach. Later, I found out they were diligently praying for the Lord to visit me. They were in the marketplace ministering. Quite interesting!

Many things changed after this incident. The most serious change was that my desire to be in the band faded. All I wanted to do was to pray in tongues. An overwhelming mantle of intercession had come upon me and I saw everything in a different light. Praying was so easy now! The crazy thing was that the word "intercession" was nowhere in my vocabulary. In fact, I didn't even know that was what I was doing. I couldn't have imagined what I was about to learn!

The Word of God was easier to read. I could actually understand it. The stories were alive and exciting. I just wanted to read the Bible and any Christian books I could find. In high school I despised reading, but God had changed that now.

My heart burned with desire to return home to Highland, New York. With each new day this desire grew stronger. I repeatedly asked, "What on earth is in Highland that I feel so strongly about returning?" I kept asking God what could possibly be there that interested Him.

In early May 1981 I heard a voice like a trumpet inside me that said, **"GO BACK TO YOUR HOME TOWN. I AM GOING TO USE YOU AS AN INSTRUMENT OF REVIVAL."** This was a very sobering experience. I knew this was a heavenly call so I didn't ask questions. I didn't even ask what "revival" meant. It was unmistakably the voice of the Lord.

A few days later my dad called. This was unusual because he normally waited for me to call. He asked when I'd be coming home, which was also unusual because he knew I wasn't due back soon. That same week, I got word that a close friend from back home had been in a serious accident and could use my help. In addition, I received a call to do a local radio commercial just three miles from Highland.

It seemed I should leave sooner than I had anticipated. I said my good-byes to the band and I was off to Highland.

During the ride back, I wondered what I would do for money. I had gotten jobs in-between singing contracts, but the band had been my primary source of income for eight years. I was willing to do just about anything, but the real question was, what was I supposed to be doing? Highland was a big contrast from Hollywood.

I wrestled with letting go of my biggest idol, my show business dream. I always thought I would be a star by age 25. I was turning 25 in a day or two and my goal was still far off. Letting go would be especially hard since my whole identity was wrapped up in singing. Who was I if I wasn't a singer? What was I created to do? It would take time before the Lord could fully reveal my true identity in Him. Little did I know, my journey had just begun.

# Chapter 2
# *A Fish Chapel?*
## *(Faith, two ice chests and $50)*

When I arrived home, I moved into an apartment above my dad's jewelry store. Dad started his jewelry shop as a young man and encouraged his kids to "be your own boss." The jewelry store was smack in the middle of town, a great location to do anything enterprising. One day, dad reminisced about the lemon-ice stand that his pop had in the alleyway years ago. He suggested I start a little stand of some sort. There would be no overhead since he owned the property. If it didn't work out, there would be no loss. In a short time what Dad suggested practically happened on its own.

I learned that the local fish market had burned down and no one in this Italian-Irish, fish-loving community was selling fish. I loved fish. I had a history of working with it— selling it, cooking it, and serving it.

One afternoon, a young woman from Florida came to mind. She had a small roadside shrimp truck. Each day she sat in a lawn chair under a big umbrella that provided shade for her ice chests. She had told me she took in about $800.00 per week. It looked quite painless to me, so I thought I'd try selling fish out of my apartment.

In three weeks, my business took off. I outgrew the apartment and moved into the alleyway. Faith, two ice chests and $50 started out this adventure. I was selling fresh fish, in the very spot where Grandpa sold his lemon ice years ago.

I needed a name for my little stand. I wanted to give Jesus first place. No hiding Him behind the scenes. I put up a big sign, right in front that read:

**"SONSHINE'Z"**
**PRAISE THE LORD!**
**FRESH FISH SOLD HERE.**

When asked why I spelled "Sun" with an "O," I would tell them, "The Son of God shines through me while I sell fish." What a riot! Known locally as a singer, here I sat under my Dad's jewelry store canopy with a backdrop of diamonds and pearls—selling fish! What an antithesis. I went from the glitter of nightclubs to the stink of fish —and, boy, both the fish and I did stink!

During my Bible reading I stumbled across *2 Corinthians 5:7. "For we walk by faith, not by sight"*

The little I could see could not be compared with what God had in mind. I had to walk in faith, because I didn't have the slightest idea why I was selling fish in an alley. Maybe this was how I would get the word out about the coming revival. Somehow, I had to tell everyone. I could tell them about my unique visitations. Or should I just be quiet and see what happened? How could I keep quiet?

I received lots of requests to sing at wedding receptions. I accepted the jobs even though I had no back-up band. I called a bass player that I knew and he happened to be putting a band together. They didn't have a singer yet, or any jobs. I asked them to work for me and we had steady weekend work for several months. This fish and singing setup got me through the summer financially while I waited to see what the Lord had in mind.

I kept up my daily jogging before I opened the stand in the morning, praying as I jogged. In the evening I rode my bicycle around the perimeters of the town asking God to bring His revival. I had a dictionary definition of the word "revival" now and I could see a glimpse of what the Lord wanted to do in Highland. My heart was heavily burdened for souls. This form of intercession was new to me. I prayed for those walking by and the owners of the local businesses as I sat in my chair waiting for customers. This kind of pray-

10

ing produced some interesting conversations. There were people that responded on the spot to the things I prayed. Literally, they would walk across the street and start a conversation with me clear out of the blue concerning my beliefs. Only I knew it wasn't "out of the blue," because of what I had just prayed. This happened constantly.

The stand was becoming pretty popular. Dad said people came from everywhere to buy Grandpa's lemon-ice. The same thing was happening with fish. It was a lot of fun, but it was hard work. I ruined lots of fish learning how to fillet. I sought experienced help but no one took me seriously. It became a real burden, so one night I asked the Lord for help. That night I had a dream with detailed instructions on how to fillet fish. It wasn't long after my divine instructions that I got the hang of filleting. Now I had another story to tell, testifying of the Father who cares for His own.

The Bible seemed more real than ever before. I believe it was because I was right out there on the sidewalk. When I read something in a Christian book or my Bible, the Holy Spirit modeled it for me. I saw needs on the faces of the people. I was like a "street counselor" listening to their problems. My heart was breaking in prayer for their needs. Much of my praying was on-site, right where the needs were.

If the streets I walked on could talk, you would have heard the cries for the lost that God put in my heart. It had only been a few months ago that all I cared about was being a star. Look what was happening to me!

I continued prayerwalking near homes and businesses where people didn't know Jesus. He cared for the lost just like He cared for me. Sometimes, it felt like my insides were coming out as I groaned and travailed for souls and for a revival of God's Spirit. What was this love I felt for them? How I wanted to understand it. Now and then my immaturity in the things of God got in the way of showing this love. How this frustrated me. Yet somehow in my "knower" I knew it wasn't about me. It was as though the Lord stood right there, reaching out to the town's people, calling them to Himself. He was in control and was choosing to use even me.

> *"For God so loved the world that He gave His only begotten Son, that whoever believes in Him should not perish, but have eternal life. For God did not send His Son to judge the world, but that the world should be saved through Him."*
>
> John 3:16-17

I thought of Jesus working with Joseph. Maybe He got to know everyone in town when they came in the carpentry shop. Maybe they watched Him mature. Maybe they knew something powerful was going on inside of Him that would one day be revealed. I imagined Jesus weeping and groaning for them to know Him as Savior when the time came.

> *And when He approached, He saw the city and wept over it, saying, "If you had known in this day, even you, the things which make for peace! But now they have been hidden from your eyes. For the days shall come upon you when your enemies will throw up a bank before you, and surround you, and hem you in on every side, and will level you to the ground and your children within you, and they will not leave in you one stone upon another, because you did not recognize the time of your visitation."*
>
> Luke 19:43

Jesus wept over the city when He gave this prophecy. His heart was broken for them. Through this scripture the Lord gave me His heart for the people of Highland.

As the customers increased so did the work—physical and spiritual. The more people I met, the more I felt the need to pray. "If Jesus would touch them just once," I thought, "they would never be the same."

I needed a prayer partner. I started asking the Lord to bring someone with the same heart and burden that I had for revival.

Business rapidly picked up. I certainly got my exercise running up and down the stairs to retrieve fish from my apartment. "There must be a better way!" I had access to the basement from the alley. Running water and a little stove were already in place. I purchased a used refrigerator to store the fish and then stretched my phone out of the apartment window into the alley. One day I was a night club singer and the next I'm the "Praying Fish Lady."

Most of my friends were confused by this career change. There were several musicians I had been praying for. One afternoon Mike drove up in a van and parked in front of the fish stand. "You're spending more time with this fish stand than your musical career, so I thought I'd bring some music to you." He put in a tape of Dixieland band music and started playing a tuba right out on the street! I laughed hysterically.

He was right. Jesus was changing my interests, and even my friends could see it! That's when I knew it was not religious deeds or my own striving but the Holy Spirit changing me. My interests changed and former priorities faded into the background. It reminded me of a song we used to sing.

> *"Turn your eyes upon Jesus, look full in His wonderful face, and the things of earth will grow strangely dim, in the light of His glory and grace."*

I could see God's fingerprints all over this tuba serenade. It was another encouragement to keep me praying. My friends were being drawn but they didn't know it was Jesus they were feeling. I kept praying for Mike and others in the music business. The church just didn't understand how to reach musicians.

Many of my friends had drinking problems. They sat in the taverns day after day. I started walking around some of the local taverns praying that Jesus would touch the people inside. For some reason, on-site prayer seemed really important.

There was a pizza parlor on the corner. Each week the owner purchased fish from me. When I told him why I spelled Sun with an "O" he said I needed to meet his daughter, who talked about Jesus like I did. She was home from Bible school for the summer to work in the pizza parlor.

"That's interesting," I thought to myself, "maybe she could be my prayer partner." When I met Margaret I knew instantly she was the answer to my prayer. She was younger than I was, sweet and soft-spoken. We had opposite temperaments, but when we prayed together, we were like one person. She was a tremendous prayer warrior and had a strong burden for the people in our town. In fact, she believed God brought her home from Bible school to pray for revival.

We were immature in the things of God, but our hearts were toward His ways. Several times each day we prayed on the phone, calling one another from the pizza parlor to the fish stand. In the evenings we prayed while walking around areas the Lord led us to. Often we prayed for someone's salvation and the next day that person would come to the fish stand or the pizza parlor. It happened fast. If it was the fish market, I called Margaret to alert her to pray. Often, she did the same.

What a great summer that was. Margaret, her cousin Joey (whom my mom brought to the Lord), and I spent our summer immersed in prayer. Strangely, that is all we wanted to do. God met us in such simplicity. Three young people finding our entertainment and excitement in prayer.

The Holy Spirit directed us to count the bars and taverns. It seemed as though they were on every corner. Some were very sleazy; a few had topless go-go dancers on the weekends. The population of Highland was less than 8,000. Why were there 25 bars in one small town? The bondage to alcohol perplexed me. I was determined to get to the bottom of this.

Every morning I walked around the parking lots and the sidewalks of three specific clubs. Day after day I asked Jesus to come with His power, to shine His light in this darkness and bring this thing called revival.

"Oh Lord, bring the bar owners, the waitresses, the bartenders and the go-go girls to salvation knowledge. Deliver them from their bondages. Nothing is impossible to You!"

Margaret, Joey and I prayed continually. No one ever modeled "appropriate prayer" for us, so we just prayed what came to our hearts. The Holy Spirit drew me into long hours of prayer and meditation on the Word. I wasn't afraid to asked God repeatedly for His help.

The Lord whispered to me,

"Rosey, you are My plow, My tiller in the Spirit, My gardener. Hook up with My Spirit and I will use you to prepare for me a highway, to make a clear highway for me to move on, to make the mountains lie flat and the crooked places straight. I will give you the bulldozers and cranes in the spiritual realm to do My work. Get yourself up on a mountain where you can see and lift your voice up mightily, lift it up and do not fear. Speak it into existence and say to Highland, 'Here is your God'!"

This helped me see that another form of intercession combined speaking out loud, prophesying, proclaiming, and declaring what God was saying and doing. I went to the high riverbanks and cliffs where I could see most of the valley. There I proclaimed God's Word over the land. I believe that speaking a prophetic word over a geographical location produces similar results as proclaiming the Word of God over a person. It allows the Holy Spirit to blow the breath of God over a whole area. Isn't that what we do in church? We speak words from the Lord over people.

In an Old Testament example, Ezekiel was set down in a valley filled with dry bones. God asked him if the dry bones could live. God was really asking Ezekiel if he had faith. After Ezekiel responded to God with faith, God told him to prophesy to the bones and when he did, they lived.

I often received revelation from the book of Isaiah so I read it often. Isaiah would say things like

> *"Clear the way for the Lord in the wilderness; make smooth in the desert a highway for our God. Let every valley be lifted up, and every mountain and hill be made low; and the rough ground become a plain, and the rugged terrain a broad valley; then the glory of the Lord will be revealed, and all flesh will see it together; for the mouth of the Lord has spoken."*
>
> *Isaiah 40:3*

What did Isaiah do with this word? Did he just write it down and hope that someday a lady in the twenty-first century would read it? NO. In the Old Testament it was common for the prophets to proclaim in the streets the things God told them. I believe Isaiah did just that.

Another strategy we used in Highland was to anoint buildings. The Israelites anointed the doorposts to keep the angel of death away and it passed by their homes. I can remember this story jumping out at me as a rhema word for our town.

We laid hands on buildings, proclaimed scripture over them and worshipped in our cars while parked in the lots. We anointed every doorway and window with oil asking God to hold back His hand of judgment. "Have mercy on them Lord. Open their eyes so they can see You."

I wish I could say we only anointed buildings the Father directed us to, but we were not mature enough for that kind of sensitivity. Looking back, the Holy Spirit directed us, but so did our fleshly zeal. In fact, some things we did were just bizarre! Thank God, He is the master teacher who allows our mistakes to train us.

There were so many little things in scripture that confirmed in my heart the need to proclaim the Word of God outside the walls of the church. Jesus did most of His ministry in the marketplace using on-site prayer and warfare. For instance, Jesus walked to the fig tree and cursed it. He didn't curse it when He was praying somewhere else. He waited until He was face-to-face with the tree. Did He know ahead of time that He was coming to this tree or did He see the Father doing something when He arrived? We don't know, but it is clear that He took action when He came on the site. He spoke out loud to the tree and the tree responded.

He gathered His disciples while passing them at their workplace. He preached, healed the sick, uplifted the broken-hearted and did most of His miracles outside the four walls of the synagogue. Marketplace ministry was common to both Old and New Testament folk because this was their way of life. They didn't have to be taught to go out into the marketplace. Every day they were out fetching water and buying food.

Other continents have far more open-air markets than the United States. Our Western culture has lost the market-place. As a result, Christians are cut off from a valuable piece of ministry. Our ministry needs to expand outside the church walls. I am convinced that God will have His way and bestow His grace on us, causing us to radically take the gospel to the marketplace!

It became evident that there was a great need to take our feet to the street in prayer and proclamation. We are to ask the Lord to show us His destiny for a certain city or nation. What is the Father saying concerning this group? What is the historical background? The Bible commands us to let our light shine in the darkness. Most of us shine our light in the light where no one notices the difference because there isn't any contrast. In the Hebraic culture, letting your light shine in the open square was customary. As Americans we need to allow the Holy Spirit to impart it. It is God's desire to bring His presence into the darkness. That is the picture I get throughout the whole Bible. They preached, mourned, prayed, fasted, prophesied, and did just about everything out in the marketplace. Why not give it a try and see what God might do?

In less than a month of praying, Tina, a former go-go dancer gave her life to Jesus. She hadn't danced for quite some time, but the club I was praying around daily was where she once worked. A month after her conversion her son gave his life to the Lord. Later he traveled with the gospel group *Truth*. Today he is in *Twila Paris'* back-up group. We never know whom our prayers will touch. The ones I least expected to reach were the ones brought into the Kingdom.

Sometimes I thought the fruit of my intercession was a result of something I did. Each time I took the glory, conviction arose while reading the Word.

> *"I am the vine, you are the branches; he who abides in Me, and I in him, he bears much fruit; for apart from Me you can do nothing."*
> *John 15:5.*

17

Jesus taught me that although I was in prayer continuously, I could not produce results apart from Him.

In the middle of town was the movie theater we went to as kids. It had turned into an XXX-rated theater. There were all kinds of perverted things going on. The pizza parlor was across the street so Margaret had a bird's eye view. Just down the block was my fish stand, right next door to one of the 25 bars. Isn't that just like the Holy Spirit to bring a bright light alongside the darkness?

Everyone knew there were questionable things going on above the theater. The police waited hoping to catch a drug deal or someone picking up a prostitute. Often the papers reported arrests for perverted acts taking place in the parking lot during the early morning hours.

Mamma Claire was the ticket teller for the movie house. She and her children lived in the upstairs apartment where a lot of the "action" took place. She loved fish and came by often. This gave me opportunity to talk to her. Most of the time I tried to encourage and love her, but I didn't pull any punches when it came to the Word of God. Even though she nodded her head, I knew she didn't understand how His love was reaching her. I only had a glimpse myself, but that glimpse was helping me see God's love for sinful people.

I finally moved my fish market indoors. It gained the nickname "Fish Chapel." That's because people told me their problems and I asked if I could pray for them.

One day Mamma Claire and I were talking. I told her that Jesus must be the Lord of our lives. It's not enough to believe, you must turn away from the world. I asked how she could keep working in the XXX-rated theater. I was direct but somehow I knew God was moving.

A few weeks later, I noticed I hadn't seen her. No one else had either. Concerned, I worked up the courage to knock on the door that led to her upstairs apartment. One of her children answered.

"Is Mamma OK?" I asked. "She is fine," he answered. At that point, Mamma came to the top of the stairs.

"Mamma Claire, I've been wondering if you were OK. No one has seen you in several weeks." She replied, "Honey, Jesus got my life and I've been knitting a blanket sitting up here praising the Lord, and watching Christian TV." I anxiously went home to call everyone I knew that had been praying for her. We were all dancing for joy. Believe it or not, Tina the ex go-go dancer played a very significant part in Mamma Claire's salvation and discipleship. Ten years later while attending a "Truth" concert, I heard a woman singing in the Spirit. When I turned around it was Mamma Claire! The road she traveled was long and hard. She has since gone home to live with Jesus forever.

After consistently praying for several years we saw the ultimate victory with the movie theater, but in the meantime some very interesting things happened.

One morning about 1:00 I shot up out of my bed. A persistent voice in my spirit said, "Now is the time to pray over the movie house." I took the chance of waking up Margaret's entire household and called her. To my surprise, she was up watching Christian television and getting the same message. The guest speaker was talking about anointing buildings and claiming them for Jesus. This was the first time we had ever heard of anyone else doing this!

In our innocence, we had been following God's heart. It was as though the Lord was saying, "Keep on doing what you are doing, I am in this more than you know."

Margaret and I decided to drive over to Joey's and see if we could wake him up without disturbing the rest of the family. Joey was asleep when all of a sudden he shot up out of nowhere, put on some clothes and opened the garage doors, only to find us pulling in the driveway. We were all stunned! When we told Joey what Margaret and I heard, he totally agreement and came along. That's what I call a divine set up.

On our way to the theater, we prayed for the Lord to shield people's eyes. We didn't want to get in any trouble or draw any unnecessary attention to ourselves. The Lord answered those prayers. About 2:00 a.m. a police car drove by just as we were openly worshipping and celebrating in faith, the closing of this place. They didn't even stop.

The Bible promises that God is a shield about us. That night we experienced it first hand. Our simple obedience paid off a few weeks later when the movie house was shut down. Unfortunately it reopened some time later and we were back to praying. It became obvious this was a battle between light and darkness. Something in me kept saying, "I refuse to quit. I have got to see this to its end."

*Ephesians 6:12 says,*

> *"For our struggle is not against flesh and blood, but against rulers, against the powers, against the world forces of this darkness, against spiritual forces of wickedness in the heavenly places."*

After we have done all, we must stand. It will come to pass! I came across many scriptures that told the saints to stand firm, press on, be sober and vigilant. The apostles were fighters. Nothing made them quit. They knew the hope of their calling.

Several times the movie house closed. Just when we thought we had the victory, it opened again. Satan certainly tried to wear us out but we were in love with Jesus and refused to quit. God gave us authority to evict spirits of darkness so there was no backing down. "Jesus shall reign in the town of Highland!"

There was a neat Jewish couple who came to the fish market, Ann and Dave. I didn't have the skill to explain their messianic heritage to them so I prayed and shared what Jesus was doing in my life. One afternoon I asked Ann if there was anything I could pray about for her. She said, "Yes," rather quickly. She needed to sell a litter of expensive puppies. This was my chance to bring Jesus on the scene. I held her hand and prayed for Jesus to help Ann sell her dogs as a token of His love for her.

After she left I continued praying for the pups and for someone who could explain the gospel to Ann and Dave. Those pups sold fast! Ann believed the prayers were the reason. I could see their hearts tenderizing. About a year later Richard, a Jewish believer, came into their lives. Ann and Dave understood Jesus as Messiah and excepted Christ. Today they still walk with the Lord.

One day it was quiet in the market so I took out my Bible. I felt a tug to look out the window and when I did the scene changed before my eyes. In the natural the street was empty but in the spirit I saw buses, cars and thousands of people. It was like a parade for a big celebrity. I blinked my eyes to be certain I was really seeing this. I instantly knew in my heart that this was revival. In this vision, the Spirit of the Lord was moving so powerfully that people were coming from all over the world to be healed and touched by God. People were in wheelchairs and on crutches. I thought, "Oh my goodness, will this really happen one day?"

Before long I started a Bible study in the market. People filled that little store until there was no more room. About the same time, I got involved in a small church that believed women should not teach. I didn't know any better so when they appointed a man to take over for me I said, "OK." As gifted as he was, the Holy Spirit lifted and people slowly left. This happened twice. In obedience to the elders I closed my Bible study. Why would God put an anointing on the group when I lead it, if the Bible tells us women are not to teach? I still didn't have God's perspective concerning women teaching Christian doctrine. I knew something wasn't right and Jesus would show me the way.

I was doing some cleaning at the store one Saturday morning. Business was usually quiet until noon. About 10:30 a.m. a man entered the store. He was about 6'4" and very husky. He wasn't familiar to me but I greeted him. He leaned over the counter and said, "What would you do if I raped you right now?" Without thinking I said, "You wouldn't be able to because I belong to Jesus." I didn't say this with pride, it just popped out of my mouth.

At first I thought he was crudely joking but he leaned over the counter and asked me the same question. This time I saw evil in his eyes. It was like Satan sent a demon into my store. I answered more seriously this time, but still firm and gentle, "In the mighty Name of Jesus no one will get raped in this store. I am protected by the blood of Jesus and His angels are stationed here to watch over me."

He seemed stunned and then asked normal questions about the fish. "I'm going to make you a fish and chips dinner," I told him. "You sit at the table by the window and

I will cook for you." I prayed in tongues asking the Lord to send another customer.

The street was very quiet. If I screamed no one would hear me and there would be no telling what crazy thing this guy might do. I made noises with the pots and sang as I cooked.

The phone was concealed behind the counter. I dialed my dad's store number and I turned on my worship music as I quietly told my dad to call the police. He said authorities were looking for an escapee from the state hospital.

As I hung up, I heard this man say, "She is protected by Jesus, I can not touch her. He is stronger than me." Demons were speaking through him and they knew they could not overpower Jesus. Just then the back door flung open. A friend that I hadn't seen in years got directions to my store and stopped in to surprise me. "Oh, I am so happy to see you," I said. Then my brother burst through the front door because my dad told him I needed help. Behind him were the police. They handcuffed the man before they took him away. I told him Jesus loved him and packed his fish "to go."

Jesus was my sword and shield that day and will be forever more. People ask, "Weren't you afraid?" Yes, I felt a strong fear. The Holy Spirit helped me not to yield, but instead to speak God's Words. Jesus taught me to believe in His power and to trust in Him more than my circumstances.

That afternoon when things were quiet again I was reading my Bible and these two scriptures just seemed to brand themselves to my heart.

> *"The Lord is my light and my salvation; Whom shall I fear? The Lord is the defense of my life; whom shall I dread?"*
>
> *Psalm 27:1*

> *"Behold I have given you authority to tread upon serpents and scorpions, and over all the power of the enemy, and nothing shall injure you. Nevertheless do not rejoice in this, that the spirits*

*are subject to you, but rejoice that your names are
recorded in heaven."*

*Luke 10:19-20*

Oh my Jesus, thank You that Your eye will ever be upon me.

As the years went by Jesus directed me to close the market. One day I just walked up to the front door and said, "Little market, this is the last day anyone will walk through your doors." The fish market stories are many. I even started a newsletter to let the customers know what God was doing. To this day, when I go back to Highland for a visit, someone always asks when I will reopen the fish market.

While writing this chapter, I called home and my dad said a man stopped in his jewelry store reminiscing about "Sonshine'z Seafood Deli." Was it the taste of fish that lingers in their mouths after all these years? Or was it Jesus, the Fisher of Men that touched them forever? There is one thing I am assured of in my heart. One day in heaven I will see many faces from the fish market. There will be people who had just been standing around listening to stories I told about Jesus that later accepted Him and received eternal life.

# Chapter 3
# *Back Home*
## *(Apprenticed by God in my hometown)*

It had been 11 years since I lived at home when my folks invited me to move back for a season. To my surprise, my mom and I began a home group. We were both privileged to be bringing lost souls into the kingdom. This group could help disciple them. God was using mom to comfort the broken-hearted of her generation. Each week our house filled with people. We had two separate telephone lines to answer all the calls.

One day I received a phone call from Tony. He was a DJ that had worked with me in clubs. Tony had opened a record Shop. I was prompted to pray for his salvation.

Of course I was looking for opportunities to share the gospel, so every few weeks I took some of my records into his store to re-sell. He wondered what happened to my singing career. This topic opened up some interesting conversations. I continued to pray for the Lord to give me freedom to share Jesus with him a little each time. A year went by and I exhausted my record supply. I left the seeds I had planted in the capable hands of the Lord.

One day I picked up the phone and it was Tony. I was quite surprised when he said, "I want to know more about this Jesus stuff. Can we meet?" He wanted to meet at a bar that was right next to the fish stand's former location. I had literally saturated that bar in prayer so I met him there. That night in the bar, Tony gave his life to Jesus. We prayed right out in the open. His life changed so drastically that his friends had a difficult time recognizing the new Tony. God had future plans for him and me to lead multiple home groups resulting in a small church plant, but neither of us had a clue at the time.

A few weeks later the doorbell rang. It was a neighbor who lived up the road from me as we grew up. After high school we had gone separate ways. Tina was recently born again but struggled with bulimia. She threw up seven times a day. Someone directed her to me for prayer. Tina accompanied me to various churches and coffeehouses where I ministered in music. She was getting a lot of prayer everywhere we went. One particular night she was baptized with the Holy Spirit, spoke in tongues and she never threw up again. It was people like Tina and Tony who began to attend our home group. They both knew a lot of people so the word about the group traveled fast.

Sometimes people would visit that we didn't know. One night several gypsies came. It wasn't unusual for the Holy Spirit to show up in extraordinary ways in these meetings. During worship the visiting ladies began having classic demonic manifestations. One woman's neck protruded and looked like a tire tube was inside her throat. She said, "I'm going to kill you."

Another hissed at me, her tongue flicking in and out of her mouth. It was long and thin like a snake's, beyond the normal human length. This spiritual dimension was quite beyond what I had experienced. Jeff, a new convert (later to be Tina's husband) spent hours with me that night praying for these women with limited results. We didn't know what to do.

God had His watchful eye upon us apprenticing us with His very own hands. Make mistakes? We sure did! The mistakes drove us to our knees. We became a group that fasted and prayed regularly for wisdom and revelation. What did we know unless God showed up to guide us?

I spent quite a lot of time with these women, as they became regulars at the meetings. I went to their homes to soak them in prayer. All of them gave their lives to Jesus, including their mother. They had many wounds, but I knew if they kept pursuing Jesus, He would reveal those things that kept them bound. I could see in the spirit the powerful calling on them to set others free. It didn't surprise me that the enemy had worked so viciously in their lives. He knew they were marked for the kingdom of God. The last I heard these ladies were all pursuing Jesus, getting free and being used by Him.

I found it interesting that the people attending our home group lived where I had been prayerwalking for several years. This encouraged me to continue praying through the streets.

About this time the Lord led me into the art of listening to promote a greater intimacy with Him. Nothing in the natural inspired this new direction, yet I was drawn into a realm I call "the quiet." It was the beginning of the discipline of listening for the Bridegroom's voice. As I sat in His Presence on the riverbank, the Holy Spirit wooed my heart towards silence, to wait for Jesus. This kind of communication with the Father, Son and Spirit would later prove to be the most powerful anchor both in my devotional life with Christ and in witnessing to others. Just silence. No music, no singing, no talking. At first I struggled, trying to bring my flesh into this silent place. As the Holy Spirit helped me, I was able to sit for longer times. Before I realized it I spent five or six hours with my heart fixed on Jesus. My flesh began to experience a place of peace I hadn't dreamed possible. This intimate time together became so enjoyable I no longer missed doing most of the talking! Jesus was becoming my best friend, my husband, my confidante and so much more. His voice resounded in nature. His ways were written across the sky. The silence captured me, filling my heart with inward heavenly music.

The Scripture became more alive than ever before. "The quiet" was changing me, causing the things of earth to grow strangely dim. I was being ruined for the things of the world. People in our meetings who had not seen results before were now experiencing deliverance. Deep places in my own life were being stirred and I would later experience the greatest freedom I could ever know.

This place of intimacy is the number one lifeline in our relationship with Jesus. The first and highest command of the Father is for us to love the Lord our God with all of our being. It is imperative to be rooted in intimacy in order to fulfill the second highest commandment, which is to love your neighbor as yourself.

Often we see the pendulum swing more toward the second commandment. As believers we were made to be lovers. Once we are filled with romance for our heavenly Bridegroom, it should begin to spill out. It's nearly impossible to fall in love with Jesus, get to know His heart for the lost, the broken-hearted, the bound and demonized and not be moved with compassion.

Our lives are created to be given away. What is there to give away that He hasn't first given us? Lord grant us a marriage between the first and second commandments, in its divine order, that we may love you and be used up for your purposes in the earth.

One day while sitting on the riverbanks the scene changed before my eyes. The banks of the river turned into walls around an ancient city. Some walls were strong and others were breached and broken. Some had watchmen in the watchtowers, others were vacant. The Lord said, "Go and build up the wall with your prayers. Your prayers are the bricks and mortar. Pray watchman into the towers and cause them to communicate with each other." The Holy Spirit drew me to Isaiah.

> *For Zion's sake I will not keep silent, and for Jerusalem's sake I will not keep quiet, until her righteousness goes forth like brightness, and her salvation like a torch that is burning. And the nations will see your righteousness, and all kings your glory; and you will be called by a new name, which the mouth of the LORD will designate. You will also be a crown of beauty in the hand of the LORD, and a royal diadem in the hand of your God. It will no longer be said to you, "Forsaken," nor to your land will it any longer be said, "Desolate;" but you will be called, "My delight is in her," and your land, "Married"; for the LORD delights in you, and to Him your land will be married. For as a young man marries a virgin, so your sons will marry you; and as the bridegroom*

*rejoices over the bride, so your God will rejoice over you. On your walls, O Jerusalem, I have appointed watchmen; all day and all night they will never keep silent. You who remind the LORD, take no rest for yourselves; And give Him no rest until He establishes and makes Jerusalem a praise in the earth. The LORD has sworn by His right hand and by His strong arm, "I will never again give your grain as food for your enemies; nor will foreigners drink your new wine, for which you have labored." But those who garner it will eat it, and praise the LORD; and those who gather it will drink it in the courts of My sanctuary. Go through, go through the gates; clear the way for the people; build up, build up the highway; remove the stones, lift up a standard over the peoples. Behold, the LORD has proclaimed to the end of the earth, say to the daughter of Zion, "Lo, your salvation comes; behold His reward is with Him, and His recompense before Him." And they will call them, "The holy people, the redeemed of the LORD;" and you will be called, "Sought out, a city not forsaken."*

*Isaiah 62:1-12*

The Lord whispered in my ear, "When the young man marries you, your marriage will be a token of the beginning of a season of revival." Knowing that my eventual marriage had prophetic significance, this word was sobering rather than exciting. I had already experienced much hardship in dating relationships; what more is coming my way?

Suddenly, I remembered my first Holy Communion. I was eight years old, dressed in a beautiful white dress with a lace veil on my head. I literally believed I was getting married to Jesus. It was a holy day in my life. There was a memorable closeness toward Jesus and I wanted to be His forever.

After the service, we marched through the streets in a procession. We were like little brides and grooms marching through the town. I turned and said to another little girl,

"This is what I'm going to do when I grow up and get married. I'm going to march through the streets and the whole town will be there."

That precious holy night ended with a severe attack on my womanhood that left me convinced that no man would ever want to marry me. Living under this stronghold of rejection I was consistently laboring in intercession for my freedom.

One Sunday morning, I took my usual walk of intercession. I was searching for a new church so I was pondering where to go to church that morning. Instead of answering that question, the Holy Spirit said, "Fast and pray." "For how long?" I asked. "Fast until I tell you to stop." I had been fasting weekly and a few times to 21 days. That morning when I read my Bible, *Isaiah 58:6-14* popped out at me.

> *"Is this not the fast which I choose, to loosen the bonds of wickedness, to undo the bands of the yoke, and to let the oppressed go free, and break every yoke. Is it not to divide your bread with the hungry, and bring the homeless poor into the house; when you see the naked, to cover him; and not to hide yourself from your own flesh. Then your light will break out like the dawn, and your recovery will speedily spring forth; and your righteousness will go before you; the glory of the LORD will be your rear guard. Then you will call, and the LORD will answer; you will cry, and He will say, "Here I am." If you remove the yoke from your midst, the pointing of the finger, and speaking wickedness and if you give yourself to the hungry, and satisfy the desire of the afflicted, then your light will rise in darkness, and your gloom will become like midday. And the LORD will continually guide you, and satisfy your desire in scorched places, and give strength to your bones; and you will be like a watered garden, and like a spring of water whose waters do not fail. And those from among you will rebuild the ancient ruins; you will raise up the*

*age-old foundations; and you will be called the repairer of the breach, the restorer of the streets in which to dwell. "If because of the Sabbath, you turn your foot from doing your own pleasure on My holy day, and call the Sabbath a delight, the holy day of the Lord honorable, and shall honor it, desisting from your own ways, from seeking your own pleasure, and speaking your own word. Then you will take delight in the LORD, and I will make you ride on the heights of the earth; and I will feed you with the heritage of Jacob your father, for the mouth of the LORD has spoken."*

*Isaiah 58:6-14*

Something told me this was going to be a longer fast than normal. That morning I met friends on their way to a new church in Poughkeepsie, New York. I went along. There were a few hundred people. I could feel the Holy Spirit settling on us. After a very intimate time of worship the pastor read from *Isaiah 58.* My heart was pounding. He said the Lord told him to call a 40-day fast for revival. I was pierced to the heart. This was the first time I would trust God for grace to fast 40 days, but not the last.

The fast hadn't even ended and it felt like there was an open heaven to bring in the lost. A chain reaction took place in our home group. Relatives of those we gathered with were giving their lives to the Lord.

As our home meetings multiplied I rented the American Legion Hall for an additional Friday night service. For purposes of unity, I invited pastors from different denominations to speak one Friday night a month. The remaining Fridays we had a variety of functions we hoped would appeal to the lost. There were game nights, movie nights, outreach dinners and the infamous, "Dance." Repeatedly the word *dance* came to us. We hesitated because of the differences in opinion concerning Christians dancing. Nevertheless, the Holy Spirit nudged us into holding a dance. So we did.

Posters went up all over town. Tony would use his DJ skills to spin records. We were all a bit nervous wondering who would come. Our apprehension led us to diligent prayer. Imagine intercessory prayer for a dance! During our prayer times God convinced us He was about to do something special.

The night of the dance two unsaved brothers showed up. Then they told us why them came. Sal, the older brother loved to go dancing. He would drive an hour and a half to Westchester to take part in the singles dance club where he was president. His plans that night were the same, but God had other ideas. Sal had seen our posters around town that week and was curious, but still had every intention of going to Westchester. However that morning his car broke down. On the wall at the auto garage was one of our posters. Sal said it seemed like something was telling him to go, so he called his brother to take him to our dance.

At this point, it was all we could to do to maintain straight faces. We invited Sal and his brother to our Tuesday evening home group. Sal gave his life to the Lord. Later we baptized him in the local reservoir. It was so cold there was a thin layer of ice on the water. Sal said he never went in the water unless it was 90 degrees. Nonetheless, he wanted Jesus to know he was serious so he plunged right in.

Sal knew scores of people and his own family was large. He had people coming from all over town. God's sovereign hand bonded Tony, Sal and me. The group nicknamed us "the God squad." We were just common folk trying to see where the Father was moving and participate with Him.

Sal soon opened his apartment for a home group. One night during prayer for revival in Highland, Ayisha Silberbush said, "Oh Lord, please come with your Holy fire and burn out the lust and perversion in our town." It wasn't like we hadn't prayed that prayer hundreds of times, only this time the town's fire siren went off. We laughed and joked with Ayisha, "The fire trucks have gone to put God's fire out." On my way home, I watched the XXX-rated movie house burn to the ground.

A local businessman purchased the remains of the site and built a well-needed municipal parking lot. Who would think a parking lot could bring glory to the name of our Lord Jesus Christ? But it did.

Moving back to my hometown was essential. Many times we have to go backwards to go forward. During this season I found going to the library to read the history of Highland and the Hudson Valley beneficial. At first I thought it was just one of my good ideas, but I rapidly changed my mind. The Lord wanted to reveal His purposes for this area to me. I learned that Highland's history included witches' covens, an important cargo landing to the Hudson Valley, and a Finny revival at the Methodist church in the 1800's that affected many people. Friends joined this research. As we prayed for more revelation it came from everywhere.

There were as many churches in Highland as there were bars, but over the years the churches became ineffective. We prayed heavily in this direction and a prophecy came forth: "There will be a great light one day on the Illinois Mountain that will pierce the darkness in the Valley."(This mountain sits in the middle of Highland).

A year later, Trinity Broadcasting Network set up a television tower on Illinois Mountain! One evening on Trinity their guest was a police officer that had tracked the witches when they left Salem, Massachusetts. He explained that they journeyed to the Illinois Mountain in Highland and settled there. Those witches dedicated Illinois Mountain and its surroundings to Satan.

This could explain why there was such a spiritual black cloud of darkness over the Hudson Valley. After this discovery, a Christian pilot flew over the mountain, anointed it with oil and dedicated it back to the Lord.

Let's look at an account in *Numbers 33:50-56:*

> *Then the LORD spoke to Moses in the plains of Moab by the Jordan opposite Jericho, saying, "Speak to the sons of Israel and say to them, 'When you cross over the Jordan into the land of Canaan, then you shall drive out all the inhabitants of the land from before you, and destroy all their figured stones, and destroy all their molten*

> *images and demolish all their high places; and*
> *you shall take possession of the land and live in*
> *it, for I have given the land to you to possess it.*
> *And you shall inherit the land by lot according to*
> *your families; to the larger you shall give more*
> *inheritance, and to the smaller you shall give less*
> *inheritance. Wherever the lot falls to anyone, that*
> *shall be his. You shall inherit according to the*
> *tribes of your fathers. But if you do not drive out*
> *the inhabitants of the land from before you, then*
> *it shall come about that those whom you let*
> *remain of them will become as pricks in your*
> *eyes and as thorns in your sides, and they shall*
> *trouble you in the land in which you live. 'And it*
> *shall come about that as I plan to do to them, so*
> *I will do to you.'*
>
> *Numbers 33:50-56*

I realized that we must go backward in order to go forward. Research was imperative to see what God's purposes were and see where Satan built his strongholds.

I discovered that the seal used over Ulster County, New York, where Highland is located, was a picture of a farmer swinging his sickle into the wheat harvest. This seal was a visual image of God's original plan for revival in the area. Obviously Satan set up strongholds to prevent it. God was going to use whosoever will to plow the land and prepare the way for His harvest.

God spoke to Moses. He told Moses if they didn't clear the land of its pagan influences, those influences would become pricks in their eyes, thorns in their sides and trouble to them in the land. That translates to me, get out the spiritual bulldozers and start building a highway for God. Give him freedom to move! Clear the way!

Most of the time when a church or a ministry begins, it is planted in what I call the thorns and the thistles. Many Christians believe that if we build, God will eventually overcome the weeds. This is not so. God wants to empower us to level the path and plow up the old foundation so He can build on fresh new spiritual soil.

Spiritual strongholds can keep the lid on all God has for our ministries. The Holy Spirit will reveal great and mighty things that we don't know if we ask Him. *(Jeremiah 33:3)* Prayer and research are two important components to receiving revelation.

I sought the Lord in this way for my own personal life. As I prayed He unveiled quite a scenario. I found out that when I was in my mother's womb, a witch put a curse on me. Once this was revealed, it took persistence and faith to see the stronghold of rejection come down. Afterwards I experienced a much greater release in every arena of my life and ministry.

God has predestined great release for us personally as well as for our cities. We are challenged to be persistent.

One of the important things I learned through my time back home was the value of commitment for the long haul. There may be some quick results, but bigger strongholds require persistent love and prayer before the final victory is experienced.

A parable in Luke helped me to hang in there when it looked like nothing was happening.

> *Now He was telling them a parable to show that at all times they ought to pray and not to lose heart, saying, "There was in a certain city a judge who did not fear God, and did not respect man. And there was a widow in that city and she kept coming to him, saying, 'Give me legal protection from my opponent.' And for a while he was unwilling; but afterward he said to himself, 'Even though I do not fear God nor respect man, yet because this widow bothers me, I will give her legal protection, lest by continually coming she wear me out.'" And the Lord said, "Hear what the unrighteous judge said; now shall not God bring about justice for His elect, who cry to Him day and night, and will He delay long over them?" I tell you that He will bring about justice for them speedily. However, when the Son of Man comes, will He find faith on the earth?*
>
> *Luke 18:1-8*

As I write, I recall many beautiful things the Lord did to apprentice me back in Highland. I believe they were direct results of the years of on-site prayer that the Lord divinely directed me to begin. The glory is all His because truthfully, I didn't even know what I was doing. He loves to use us when we don't have a clue. He is the potter and we are the clay.

My hope is that these stories make known the value of consistent, on-site prayer, fervent intercession and historical research. Try it in your geographic arena and see what happens!

Was my work for the Kingdom completed in Highland? These things He accomplished from those years of intercession:

- There were no longer topless Go-Go girls in the bars.

- Several bars closed; most of the remaining ones became the eat-in type.

- The wife of a bar owner got saved; his sister also got saved and married a man who later became a pastor in the Hudson Valley.

- Scores of people came to Jesus and were baptized in pools, lakes and bathtubs. They brought friends, cousins, brothers, sisters, etc.

- My own sister rededicated her life and saw many of her friends get saved.

- We had unusual favor with the mayor and city officials.

- Relationships were restored within families.

- Spirit-filled Christians moved here from all over the country.

- Home groups and new churches sprang up.

- After praying around the schools for some time, a spirit-filled Superintendent was hired and worked in Highland for 10 years.

- Lives were completely changed. People were delivered from drugs, alcohol addiction, eating disorders and demons.

- Many of us experienced divine provision.

- Today Tony is an ordained pastor living with his family in Middletown, New York.

- Margaret, a young drug addict, was found sleeping on doorsteps after her mother committed suicide. She got saved, baptized, delivered, healed, married a wonderful Christian and works as a church secretary.

- We prayed for Sal to get a bed. He got five! He began giving them away. To this day there is a "bed anointing" on Sal. More people have given him beds than anyone I have ever met, and He has given them to those in need.

I spent seven years on the banks of the Hudson River. Now when my husband and I go back to New York, he knows the river is the first place I go. Of all the ten countries we have had the privilege to enjoy, my favorite place to be with Jesus is still on the banks of the Hudson River in Highland, New York.

I can not attest that thousands came to the Lord in Highland, but I believe they will. We *prepared the way for the Lord* and He will visit there with revival as He promised.

Again, may I encourage you? Be in it for the long haul. Never doubt that you are on the winning side, even while you are being persecuted. It's important to really get hold of who we are in Christ and who is living inside of us.

# Chapter 4

# *Who Is Living In You?*

**O**ver the years I have come to a fuller realization of Who is living inside me. The Lord helped me comprehend that I was not only a born-again, blood-bought believer, but that the Hope of Glory, the Holy Spirit, the living God of the universe is living inside me. As a result, I understand prayer in a different dimension. This is the reason my prayer life changed from simply asking to declaring, decreeing, and prophesying the things of God into existence. I got a glimpse of how God sees me and I believe He wants to use me to be His instrument of revival through the vehicle of prayer.

Having a history in the music business, I understood that an instrument is played by its owner. I knew that if I were the instrument, I needed to yield to the One who plays through me. The master of the instrument makes the choice of the tune. The instrument does not.

You may ask, "how can I pray boldly before the throne of God if I don't feel bold? How can I pray and believe, if I feel inadequate?" Head knowledge has to become revelation and then tangible daily experience so we can see Who prayer releases.

Prayer releases the hand of the God of the universe. As I meditated on this thought, I saw that prayer had absolutely nothing to do with who I am or who I'm not. It had everything to do with who He is. My part is to yield to the melody that He selects.

We are God's hands and feet on the earth. The Bible tells us in *Colossians 1: 26-27;*

> *"This is the mystery which has been hidden from past ages and generations; but has now been manifested to His saints, to whom God willed to make known what is the riches of the glory of this mystery among the Gentiles, which is Christ in you, the hope of glory."*
>
> *Colossians 1: 26-27*

Paul concludes in verse 29, *"...and for this purpose also I labor, striving according to His power, which mightily works within me."*

Paul knew who was working in and through him and as a result, neither his flesh nor the attacks of man' hindered him. He knew God was bigger than anything that would come his way, even intense persecution. Here are some additional verses showing Christ's indwelling presence in us:

> *"I have been crucified with Christ; and it is no longer I who live, but Christ lives in me...."*
>
> *Galatians 2:20*

> *"And the glory which Thou hast given me I have given to them; that they may be one, just as We are one; I in them, and Thou in me...."*
>
> *John 17:22-23*

Jesus himself said, **"I in them."**

The Apostle Paul asked the Corinthians a sobering question;

> *"Do you not know that you are the temple of God, and that the Spirit of God dwells in you?"* (Did they know it? Do we know it?) *"If any man destroys the temple of God, God will destroy him, for the temple of God is holy and that is what you are."*
>
> *1 Corinthians 3:16*

Paul helped the Corinthians understand that they were now the temple of the God of Abraham, Isaac and Jacob. Listen closely, as a Christian you are now a living Holy of Holies. The presence of the awesome Creator of the earth now dwells in our "temples," our earthen vessels. Can you say "Yes" and believe it? Yes, Yes and Yes again! We have got to get a revelation that we are the very sanctuary of the Holy Spirit. We are filled with God!

The God of the universe absolutely adores you enough to put his own Spirit in your body. This is so you can be side-by-side with Him bringing forth His purposes on the earth and so you can know how greatly you are loved. Jesus said it was because the Father loved us, that He sent His Spirit to dwell in us. We have the divine personality of this Holy Spirit living in us.

We may think we are nothing, but we are something. God looked at you and said, "I'm going to put my Spirit in you." When the devil tells us we are worthless our response should be, "I can't be worthless if the Holy Spirit lives in me. I must be something." Think about it. We must be something for God to love us this much. He came and got us and brought us to Himself. We think that we found the Lord. No, God found us! He searched for us and bought us with His own blood!

This understanding makes me want to leap and sing for joy! My brain tilts when I think of how unfathomable this truth is. Oh, how we need to take hold of this and believe we are joint-heirs with the King of Kings. We are His Bride, and He has given us His very own Spirit to help us explode in love and endure to the end. Lovers just love to be together building things side-by-side.

In the Old Testament, people did not have the Holy Spirit abiding in them, they had the Holy Spirit upon them. Yet look at the results of their prayers—they split the sea, beheaded giants and took down Jericho. They simply interceded by standing on their covenant rights. We New Testament believers not only have the Holy Spirit fall upon us, but He abides within us.

Unfortunately, many believers don't know what that really means. In the Old Testament, His presence and power dwelt inside the Ark of the Covenant. When the Israelites went to battle, they always sent the Ark in front of the army. Time after time God sent their enemies into confusion. Sometimes the enemy even killed their own men. It was never the number of soldiers, nor their fighting skills that won the battle. God, by His Spirit, won the battles the Israelites faced with His awesome power that indwelt the Ark.

Today the cross of Jesus Christ makes a way for us to come boldly before the throne. We don't have to wait for the Ark to come to our town, we have the same power of the Ark living on the inside of us; our bodies are New Testament arks.

*Hebrews 8:6* says that New Testament believers are under a *better covenant.* That's an understatement! We have the Helper, the Comforter, the One who can lead us into all truth living inside of us. Every gift of the Holy Spirit lives inside our very being.

We need to tap into this revelation and allow the Holy Spirit's ministry to fully come forth. We need to become co-laborers with the Holy Spirit and get to know Him. The more we know Him, the more we can see where the Father is moving, the more we do what the Father is doing, the more fruit we will bear in the things of the Spirit.

When God desires to move on the earth, He looks for a human who will agree with Him and His Word. He wants an instrument to play through. Our response to Him enables us to speak the things of the Kingdom on earth. *1 Corinthians 3:9* tells us we are God's fellow workers. We are laboring together with Christ Jesus. He made us for His pleasure and He takes pleasure in doing things with us. That's why we are each called to do specific ministries.

From our perspective it is frustrating to wait for God to show up, but really, He is patiently waiting for us to step out and take hold of the power inside us. It perplexes me that He uses earthen vessels. We barely understand His passion for us and we barely understand His desire to partner with us. He likes us; He likes doing things with us.

Why is it so hard for us to partner with this divine nature living inside us? I have listed five reasons:

1. I believe for some of us it's the issue of independence. We naturally want to do it ourselves and receive the credit, because credit feels good. Independence may ask for God's ways, but it resists His daily friendship. Our Western culture entices us to do our own thing, in our own way. This causes difficulty in our natural relationships, how much more our relationship with the Holy Spirit?

2. For others, partnership is blocked by fear of intimacy. The Western mindset has built a fear of intimacy in the very core of our being. It has caused us to become comfortable with just a little touch from God instead of the long embrace He desires to give us. Jesus wants to embrace us. Do we know that?

3. For some, the wrong perspective of humility blocks partnership. Focusing on our weaknesses is not humility. Humility is knowing that we are weak and He is strong in us, in spite of our weakness. I constantly remind myself that I can't do anything without the Holy Spirit. How can I play the instrument if I am the instrument? I need to yield so the Holy Spirit can bring forth the melody the Father desires to play. I long to be used to play a sweet melody to my lover the King, or sound the alarm to muster the troops.

4. In addition to these reasons, it's sad that so often we are just too busy to spend time with the Lord. Our time is spoiled by the cares of this world, which are often unimportant.

5. Above all, I believe that the most prominent reason we fail to partner with God is simple unawareness. I rarely hear balanced teaching on the partnership of the divine nature, which lives inside us. It's as if there is a big stronghold robbing the Word before it reaches us. As a result we never internalize the clear message.

The enemy knows that if we could just get a tiny glimpse of who is living inside us there would be no stopping us. He keeps us captivated by our own limitations, fears and inadequacies, while having a field day laughing at us. That's why there is such a fight to keep us from understanding this mystery.

In *1 Corinthians 6:19*, Paul asked a question similar to *1 Corinthians 3*:

> *"Or do you not know..."* (Paul is hammering away at those things that assault the truth. He realizes they haven't gotten it yet.)"*...that your body is the temple of the Holy Spirit who is in you, whom you have from God and that you are not your own?"*
>
> 1 Corinthians 6:19

Do we know who is living on the inside of us? Do we realize that every gift of the Holy Spirit resides in our very being? Do we realize that we are not our own, we are *His instruments?* Has the church at large really comprehended this truth?

Are we making disciples and transferring to them the understanding that they are now partakers of a divine nature? That is what happens when we are born again. We receive a new nature, the divine nature of our heavenly Bridegroom. Wow! Can you believe what a great love God the Father loved you with, to send his only Son to die on the cross for you so you could partake in this heavenly calling?

We must *"Guard through the Holy Spirit who dwells in us, the treasure which has been entrusted to you"* (2 Timothy 1:14).

What is this treasure? This treasure is the living Presence of God. We are living Holy of Holies, living, breathing arks of the covenant. Wherever we go, God's Spirit goes. Even when we are not conscious of it, our feet take the presence of God into the world. The lost can feel the same power and love that we feel in the congregation of the saints.

In *Galatians 4:19*, Paul said he was in labor for them until Christ was formed in them. We are a temple that is not made with human hands. That is part of the great mystery even the angels marvel at. We are a living building being built into a House of Prayer. When Jesus said, "My house shall be called a House of Prayer," was He referring to an actual building? No, the house and the temple are our bodies.

You and I have the Holy Spirit dwelling inside us to teach us, comfort us, guide us, convict sinners, change impossible circumstances, explode our hearts into the love of God, raise the dead, split the sea, bring the walls down, stand in the gap, move mountains, heal the sick, cast out demons, love the unlovely, endure hardships—the list goes on and on.

This should encourage us to go into our neighborhoods and proclaim to the captives that this is the favorable year of the Lord! Here is one of my favorite declarations over my neighborhood:

> This is the favorable year of the Lord for you. The Spirit of the Lord God is more than upon me, He is within me. I declare that the afflicted on this street will hear the good news of the glorious gospel. I proclaim liberty to the captives and freedom for the prisoners from Satan's clutches. Lord, comfort all that mourn. Grant them a garland of praise instead of ashes and the oil of gladness instead of mourning.
>
> Let the people in this neighborhood praise You and be called oaks of righteousness, the planting of the Lord, that You may be glorified in this neighborhood.

The glory of God flows out of us through prayer. I believe we can prophesy the Word of God over an area and it will happen. Sometimes sooner than expected. Why? Because when we speak forth God's Word, the things He created can come into order. We are calling things that are not yet visible into existence. God already created them; we just have to call heaven and earth together. That's the believer's authority. God created it and we tell it to do what God created it to do.

I believe that speaking God's Word creates pockets of hope in the atmosphere which penetrates the darkness, so that the lost and (believers too) can actually sense it and be drawn to God. When I get to heaven, there will be people that I never knew by name who were set free from bondage by my prayerwalking.

While I ride my bike or drive home from work, I call out; "this is the favorable year of the Lord for you. You shall be saved in Jesus' Name." We don't realize we create pockets of hope this way. But one day, we will find out.

Once we start to take hold of this truth we will join together with the Holy Spirit to pray *city-sized prayers* and see our neighborhoods and cities filled with the glory of the Lord as the waters cover the sea *(Isaiah 11:9)*. We will see how broad God is and it will enlarge our vision for prayer. Once we have the vision, it won't matter how insignificant we feel. We will focus on how vast God is. Having His vision keeps us praying.

We will put off preoccupation with self and begin to accept the fact that if God's Spirit lives inside us and goes where we go, then we simply cooperate with Him and He can explode with His love where ever we are.

When I go grocery shopping, I let God know I am available. I talk to Him like I would to my friend: "Lord, if there are people You want to talk to, help me to see who they are and what You're doing so I can cooperate." This simple prayer has opened up a multitude of divine appointments.

Once I did an experiment. Before going out, I told the Holy Spirit I was available. He used me, even putting others in my path to bless me. When I didn't volunteer, it was just another shopping trip. The scripture says that we have not because we ask not. We are commanded to ask. God's principles work, even in the produce aisle!

I don't own a washing machine because I've discovered the Laundromat is a ministry hot spot! As I stuff my towels in the washer, I let the Holy Spirit know I'm available and many times, even before the rinse cycle, someone brings up the subject of God. I hold back laughter while thinking, "Go for it, Holy Spirit." Sometimes as I read a Christian book, the Holy Spirit will inspire others to ask questions and the doors swing wide open. For me, as people join in these conversations about Jesus, the laundromat seems like church.

Once I asked the Holy Spirit if my laundromat ministry days were over because nothing was happening. I'd forgotten to make myself available. That night I prayed and a young woman asked what I was reading. As we talked I invited her and her husband to church. They became believers and it all started at a laundromat. God is so cool.

Simply by staying available to the Holy Spirit while doing laundry, I have led many to Christ and the unchurched to church.

One of the Holy Spirit's jobs is to convict people of sin. He is convicting them of sin wherever we go, whether we know it or not. If we cooperate we are available when divine appointments cross our path. If we are unbelieving or unaware, we quench the Spirit. Why? Because we do not cooperate with the work He is already doing.

For example, for no apparent reason a waitress gets belligerent. You don't realize it but she is trapped in sin. The Holy Spirit, living on the inside of you, is convicting her. She feels guilty and ashamed. You can snap back at her, or you can put up your spiritual antennae and ask the Lord to give you a compassionate word.

God loves releasing His gifts in the marketplace. He wants to love sinners through us. We can participate just by asking what He wants us to do. It's His desire to cleanse and put His divine nature in them, too.

*Romans 5:5* tells us that *"...the Love of God has been poured out within our hearts through the Holy Spirit who was given to us."* God's love is given to us and we need to ask the Holy Spirit when, where and how to release it. More times than not, God has given me a kind word for a snarling waitress. It releases tension and momentarily draws her into the love of God.

A prophetic word helps sinners see God's love for them even while they are in their sin. Remember that it's God's kindness that leads people to repentance. No one ever fell in love with the *big hammer God in the sky.*

I wish I could say I never missed it, but I am becoming more sensitive to the Holy Spirit in the marketplace each day. Keep in mind friendship with God is imperative.

A few of us were prayerwalking a neighborhood. I noticed a woman go to her mailbox. As she walked towards the house I had an impression we should ask her if she had anything we could pray for her. She told us she was going to a doctor that Friday and would appreciate prayer.

As she spoke I saw a picture of a lump in a body part and her lying on a bed crying. I asked her if what I saw was applicable to her condition and she said it was. This helped me boldly ask if we could pray for her on the spot.

When she agreed, we prayed the lump would dissolve and that the love of God would comfort her. I took note of the house she lived in and returned two weeks later to see how things went. I rang the doorbell and before I could ask if she remembered who I was, she wrapped her arms around me tightly and thanked me, explaining that the lump had disappeared and she no longer needed surgery.

Start crying out to God for help to tap into this revelation of Who is living on the inside of you. Ask Him to open the eyes of your heart, so that you may be enlightened to know what are the riches of the glory of His inheritance in the saints *(Ephesians 1:18)*. Ask God for a fresh glimpse of how He sees you, how He made you and what you're predestined to do for Him.

Get to know God. Get to know the Holy Spirit. Be as desirous of Him as He is of you. Leap with Him on the mountains. Run with Him over the hills. Subdue the earth with Him. Rule and reign with Him. You are joint heirs with Jesus. We are small, we are weak, we can't produce lasting results without Him, but we can yield to this awesome power inside us. When you don't know what to pray, pray in the Spirit. When you feel intimidated, say, "Holy Spirit release your confidence within me."

The Bible tells us to be strong in the Lord and the power of His might. It's His strength that will carry you through. He promised to be with us to the end and He's not like men that He should lie. We can't do it without Him, but we can yield our hearts, minds, ways, plans, ideas and all that we are to Him and He will gladly make Himself strong on our behalf. When persecution comes, you will be able to stand by His might.

*2 Corinthians 6:16* says, *"I will dwell in them and walk among them; I will be their God and they will be my people."* The first time we see God walking with man is in Genesis. God loved His creation and walked and talked with them. Now He is in us and wants to walk among His people including the lost to bring them to salvation.

This is why it's important to take your feet to the street, to the laundromats and grocery stores. It's a prophetic drama of what God wants to do. Once you realize God's love for you and accept that His love dwells in you by the Holy Spirit, you can't help but want to cooperate with God wherever you go.

Everything you could ever need is living on the inside of you because God designed it that way. When you received the Holy Spirit you received the whole package. You get to pray boldly and confidently because of who He is in you and who you are in Him. It's not us having the right words, it's not us being confident enough, and it's not us becoming skilled enough. It's all about releasing the God of the universe who is living inside you. You are His beloved. We must have faith that He wants to work His earthly purposes through us. We get to hook up with the greatest prayer meeting going on day and night. It starts through us by the Holy Spirit to Jesus, then right to the throne of the Father!

Jesus ever lives to make intercession for us. *"...as He is, so also are we in this world" (1 John 4:17)*. Let's join in this eternal prayer meeting that is taking us right to the threshold of the great wedding supper of the Lamb. Get to know who is living on the inside of you and put your faith in Him. *"...greater is he who is in you than he that is in the world" (1 John 4:4)*. This is a part of the great mystery, *Christ in you the hope of Glory.*

Lord, reveal this mystery to us all!

# Chapter 5
# BUS 23
## *(God shows up at the bus garage)*

The Holy Spirit repeatedly told me I would go into full-time ministry with full-time pay. It looked as though I would work for my church since I was pastoring a prayer ministry there.

I was a bit puzzled and extremely humbled when He told me to drive a school bus. I tried to find reasons why this job wasn't for me, but as usual, God was inflexible with His plans. On February 10, 1988, I was hired as a school bus driver in a small New York town, a few miles from Highland. When summer came I took a vacation to attend a Vineyard ministry conference in California.

Before leaving, my prayer group shared their impressions concerning this trip. They told me there would be three divine appointments that would significantly impact and expand my prayer ministry.

I did in fact have three divine appointments. Each one was a pastor with a heart for prayer. The most profound meeting I had was with Mike Bickle, a pastor from Grandview, Missouri, a Kansas City suburb. After the conference God divinely provided for me to visit his church. I encountered some very prophetically gifted people who gave language to several aspects of my life that up until that time no one could explain. I thought for sure God was about to direct me to move there, but He didn't just then.

What I didn't know was that the Lord would move me to Kansas City seven years later. Until then I would return to my new job as a bus driver and be faithful to the mission set before me.

After a year or two of driving I got a glimpse of what God was doing at my job. I saw many opportunities for prayer with 70 employees in the transportation department. I had started out as a substitute driver and also drove activity trips. This opened up the opportunity to be in everyone's bus at one time or another. I prayed and anointed all the seats each time I got in a new bus. Since this on-site prayer had brought surprising results in Highland, why not try it again? I believed that God would make Himself known among the drivers and students that rode on these buses.

The Holy Spirit revealed to me that bus drivers touch just about every home in town each day. God's heart began to unfold. In my heart I thought, "If they only knew Jesus, we could touch every home in the area with the presence of God each day." Wow!

Needs outside the church are greater than that inside. We as believers have many needs but we know we will be with Jesus for all eternity. The lost are bound for eternal torment, forever absent from the presence of God. This thought kept me diligently praying for the students, their families, and my fellow employees.

Eventually I obtained my own bus route along with cleaning the bus garage offices in-between runs. As I dusted and vacuumed, I prayed over every inch of that building. I invited the Holy Spirit to live and dwell on this bus lot and to love on those people in ways they couldn't imagine. The Devil was mad and started showing his ugliness but through the grace of God, I remained steadfast, believing and praying for God to visit.

As Christians we must believe the Word of God with simplicity. Satan is the god of this world and does his best to throw some punches to knock us out. Remember that getting punched is inevitable when we are in the ring, but if we fight with the might of the Lord we don't have to stay down.

The Apostle Paul encourages us to stand against the wiles of the Devil. Resist him and he will flee. Don't back down. Don't let him wear you out; you wear him out. *Ephesians 6:10* tells us to *"...be strong in the Lord and in the strength of His might."* It's all Him. We are just available vessels that His power works through. Always call on the

Holy Spirit for help. He will empower us in all our circumstances.

Sometimes whle reading in the breakroom, drivers would ask me about my beliefs. They said there was something about me that led them to think I was *into religion*.

The word "religion" was perfect for striking up conversations. My standard reply was, "I hope I'm not religious, but I am striving for a right relationship with Jesus." The inevitable next question was often, "What's the difference?"

It was divine entertainment watching the Holy Spirit move and stir up questions in their hearts. The groundwork was done in prayer. I would plow the ground, drop the seeds, water them with my intercession and wait for the harvest. This went on for almost two years.

I was in my thirties, still single and waiting on the Lord for a mate, convicted and convinced that dating wasn't for me. If it was God's choice I was prepared to live a celibate lifestyle; in fact, I diligently prayed for the gift of celibacy. If God did have a mate for me, he would find me clinging close to Jesus. I believed it was God's job to pick a man for me and then be my Father and arrange the marriage.

It wasn't always easy to live what I believed, so I don't say this lightly, but the Holy Spirit was truly my comforter and helped me in my times of weakness. I was about my Father's business and having a pretty good time. Please, don't let my belief condemn yours, but I was set firmly at that time and still am today that this is God's way for His children.

The mechanics in the bus garage teased me royally because I didn't date. They were good guys, but my lifestyle was just too peculiar for them. They would call me an *old maid* and tell me I was never going to get married if I didn't make myself available. I had to guard my heart against receiving their jests. At times their remarks challenged my faith, and I wondered if what they were saying had any truth in it.

Lifting up my voice, I'd sing about Jesus right in the parking lot while I washed my bus. My favorite song was "My redeemer is faithful and true." The song implies that we can rest and believe in a God who keeps His promises.

I didn't hesitate to sing out because I knew how powerful praise is when emotions are contrary to the word of God. Those songs lifted my soul and I was filled with belief again.

They were watching me, watching my life, listening to what I said. My prayers were tenderizing their hearts.

The Bible tells us in *2 Corinthians 4:4,*

> *"in whose case the god of this world has blinded the minds of the unbelieving, that they might not see the light of the gospel of the glory of Christ, who is in the image of God."*

Day after day I prayed that the blinders would be lifted so they could see the glory of Christ Jesus. There was a fight going on in the heavenlies and I was battling for their souls.

Most of my praying was and is in tongues. The Holy Spirit knows more than I do about every situation, so I hook up with Him. The Spirit helps us to pray the rhema word of God. In other words, He prays through us exactly what is needed for each situation.

Read Romans chapter eight. It's an important chapter about praying with the help of the Holy Spirit. I believe we pray too much in our own understanding. The Holy Spirit was sent to help us because we need help. He knows God the Father's mind and knows how to bring the Kingdom of Heaven right here to earth. The Holy Spirit will lead us into what to pray in English too. The results are astounding.

For two and a half years, I anointed seats and offices and prayed in tongues. I saw tokens of answered prayer but nothing major. However, there was one thing that happened that totally changed me. God did an important work in my heart, changing my entire outlook toward homosexuals. I had a problem trying to love gays and lesbians with the kind of love God had for them. I didn't realize it until I came face-to-face with the ugliness in my own heart.

The town we were in was filled with new-age bookstores, witchcraft, and bizarre sexual lifestyles. It was a college town still stuck in a 1960's mindset. Jill, a woman from work, invited me to go skating. While skating, a word of knowledge for her came to me. I saw two circles joined together like wedding rings. They were slowly torn apart like a divorce or the death of a relationship. Then I could feel her heart like it was my own. She was aching on the inside. This is called *empathic intercession*. I asked her if she was married or recently in a relationship that ended or if her boyfriend had died. She laughed and said, "Rosey, I'm a lesbian." I was a bit shocked.

I tried to explain what a *word of knowledge* was and how God shows us things about others to let them know. He loves them and wants to heal them. I apologized thinking I must have been off this time. She said, "You weren't off at all. I lived with a woman for many years and she recently died."

I struggled with God giving me this word. The real truth was I couldn't believe He wanted to heal her broken heart. After all, she was a lesbian. My lack of understanding the ways of God was at war with His heart in that moment. Let me say that I believe the Biblical teaching - that homosexuality is a sin and God hates it- but I don't think we even have a glimpse into the love God has for the people stuck in this sin. I personally did not.

On our way home we talked about her childhood. She had had several stepfathers. More than anyone I had ever met. Most of them were in the military. If you knew about the life of most military children your heart would break. When she shared her stories, I saw how the enemy shattered her image of a father, or any man, for that matter.

My heart was deeply convicted that I needed to do some serious repenting. "How did she survive all the emotional trauma," I wondered? The Holy Spirit showed me even more than she was sharing.

That night I could not sleep. Everything inside me was gripped with a prayer burden for her. I moaned and travailed most of the night. It seemed as if I was praying evil spirits off of her mind and plowing a clear path for the word of God to reach her. It would take a miracle from God to untangle the web of hurt she was in. Her picture of what a father is was distorted. Her view of God was set in cement. Only He could set her free.

After this night in prayer, God imparted to me a kind of love for homosexuals that I never thought possible. I realized Satan had robbed them of their identity. Jesus wanted to heal and restore what the devil had stolen. Oh, how Jesus loves them and wants us to love them too.

I became Jill's friend. One day she commented how nice it was to have a friend that was straight. She explained that she was always concerned that her friendships with other lesbians would be misinterpreted as attraction. She felt like she could trust me. This broke my heart again. I thought of all the women friends I trusted and loved and couldn't imagine how she must have lived void of these wonderful relationships. In the natural, it didn't look as though I made much progress with Jill, but I knew God had planted seeds in her heart that would one day take root.

(I will share more about Jill later.)

I discovered another co-worker was also a lesbian. She shared she had been raped by a stranger early in life and ended up hating men. As Christians we struggle walking through such horrible trials. Just imagine how awful it must be for the ones who have no knowledge of God and His ability to heal them. Lord, help us to see with Your eyes and feel with Your heart!

God used me with co-workers and also with my riders. I had been driving Larry, a four-year-old with Down's Syndrome, who was hard to manage. He was deaf in one ear and could hardly speak, making communication difficult between us. There was no aide available for my bus so it was challenging to keep him seated. Daily I prayed for wisdom. After speaking with Larry's parents and teachers,

I found out he could communicate through sign language. He did fine in school because they could sign to him, but on the bus he would get frustrated and even throw his shoes at me. It broke my heart that I couldn't communicate with him.

I decided to take a sign language course. The course was full but I had a divine appointment with the teacher and she made room for me. Patty, the teacher was a very compassionate deaf woman. I was able to minister to her and some college students during the semester. The course opened my heart to better understand a deaf world I hadn't known existed.

After a couple classes I was able to sign a few words to Larry. If you could have seen his face, tears would have rolled down yours. He was so excited that I could communicate with him. In a short period of time many of his behavioral difficulties stopped on the bus. The neat thing about Larry was he liked me to sing and sign songs. Imagine me driving, singing and signing. I told him about Jesus and he signed back. For the three years he rode my bus I planted some good seed in his heart for the Holy Spirit to water.

Because of Larry's remarkable improvement, children with similar disabilities were assigned to my bus. This meant I had more mothers with whom to converse. It was a fun bus and each child turned their heart toward Jesus.

In the spring of 1990, another Patty was hired as a driver. I didn't pay special attention to her but I did include her in my prayers. We chatted occasionally, but had no involved conversations. I was not aware that two years prior, she was drawn to the Lord through Christian television but nothing significant had happened spiritually for her. Soon, however, Patty would play a very strategic part in what the Lord was about to do at the bus garage.

June came and only a few of us had summer runs. Things would be quiet on the work site until September. A very interesting stirring was going on in my personal life. During an all-night prayer meeting in July, Don and Lois, my pastors, prayed that God would send me a husband. About a month later, I met Bill, the man who would soon ask for my hand in marriage. The spotlight began to shine on me at work when I mentioned there was the possibility of a man coming into the picture.

It was in the fall that the Lord touched down and began to show up by surprise on my job and in my life. Gail, a Jewish believer, and Deborah, whom I had brought to Jesus during the Highland years, had been hired as a bus driver and my aide, respectively. With all three of us on the same job, a lot of prayer was going up.

In May of 1991, I posted an invitation on the bulletin board at work for "whosoever will" to come to my wedding, literally arranged by my Father in Heaven. I knew God was about to do something mighty in the spiritual realm and I didn't want anyone left out. The mechanics, the drivers, all the parents and students had watched me for three years standing firm, waiting for God's timing. He was about to allow them see His word come to pass, first-hand.

The day of my wedding came. The ceremony was held in the Methodist church that sat exactly in the middle of Highland, where a Finney revival occurred in the 1800's. Worship like that never flooded the streets of Highland. People came out of the surrounding businesses to see what was going on. The church was filled with students, parents, co-workers, relatives, church friends, and even people I didn't know.

A young woman that I had never met came out of the pizza parlor across the street. She shouted to me that everything looked beautiful. I invited her to come and enjoy the ceremony. "Oh, I would love to but I'm not dressed properly," she pointed to the old jeans she was wearing. We were shouting back and forth across the street. I shouted, "I'm the bride. It's my wedding. I say come as you are."

At the conclusion of the ceremony while we were greeting our guests, she came to thank me. I held her hand and she began to cry and tell me how touched she was by the wedding. Right on the spot I led her to Christ. It was the best wedding present I received! Others were healed and two lesbians were deeply moved and spent the entire wedding in tears. There was an altar call and several others gave their lives to Jesus. It was a glorious day!

As the wedding procession went through town to the reception - held on the banks of the Hudson River (where else?) - I remembered my first Holy Communion 25 years before. I was 35 years old now. Satan fought hard against this day, but when it was God's time, nothing and no one could stand in His way.

After the wedding things began to break loose at my job. One morning Deborah struck up a conversation with Patty. Patty told us she had been watching Christian television for two years. Helen, another driver, was drawn to our conversation. I could see the harvest nearing. These ladies were hungry so I offered to teach them. Soon they came to church and I had the privilege to lead them to Christ. Patty opened her home for a Bible study in-between our bus runs. Gail, our Jewish Believer led worship and even helped train Patty to lead also.

More people from work were coming to church with us. I remember one Sunday 16 of us all sat together. Don and Lois Richter were superb pastors. They oversaw my baptizing several of these ladies in the college pool on a cold February evening.

I had learned the value of on-site prayer, so we met regularly in my bus to pray. As we prayed for a specific driver standing in the parking lot, that driver would be drawn to the bus to ask what we were doing. It was just like the fish stand. Praying on-site was simply awesome. We could see the Holy Spirit move right before our eyes. This fueled our prayers. We were all praying together for students, teachers, parents, fellow employees, and even the school administration. I was no longer praying alone.

One morning during a prayer meeting in my bus, a lesbian co-worker came to the door. I saw her eyes fill up with tears. She stumbled into the bus and hit the floor crying, "I need Jesus." The Spirit of God was moving powerfully. I had the privilege of leading her and her friend to Jesus and I baptized them in a swimming pool.

Helen had a difficult week of warfare and was getting worn out. Students were fighting on the bus, several broke bones, all sorts of bizarre things occurred. I encouraged her to pray through her bus, anoint it with oil, break the power of the enemy and release God's angels of protection. When she did, the storm calmed. Anointing our buses became a habit because when we did it, the hearts of our students opened wide to Jesus. I was in the middle of what I called a "mini-revival" again.

Bill, my new husband, was in the army. It was always in the back of my mind we could be ordered to leave the state or even the country. With sweet Jesus touching us at work, I couldn't bear the thought of moving.

Government orders were issued. We were reassigned to Germany. I was certain this was straight from the pit of hell. Helen was also struggling with a move. She had married a man from Iceland, her home country. Employment in his field was drying up in our area, but was plentiful there. No matter how much we prayed these moves were not thwarted.

Suddenly, I needed to prepare to move overseas. Everything I owned needed to be packed and moved to Maryland with Bill's belongings at his U.S. duty station. After we unpacked the army would repack and ship it all together to Germany. Leaving my dreams for revival behind was all so hard to accept. Nevertheless, I was now the property of the United States Government and the process ahead was irrevocable unless the King of Glory stepped in.

God was still moving mightily at work. A shaking took place in that school district. People in high positions were literally shaken from their jobs and godly people took their places. Someone had to keep pressing into God on the behalf of this job-site. I knew that Patty was the one.

Before I left, I passed the mantle to her, and as I write this chapter years later, Patty still holds her position there as a driver, reaping the fruit of those years of prayer. She is also part of a church plant birthed from the church we all attended. They are prayerwalking, researching the history of the area and preaching the good news of Jesus Christ. God will use them to bring the lost and broken into His arms again

It was now seven years since I had heard the voice like a trumpet calling me to be an instrument of revival. I spent those seven years diligently in intercession, mostly outside the walls of the church. God had been faithful. Many souls had come into the kingdom, were healed, discipled and changed. The Kingdom of God truly does suffer violence and we must violently take it by force *(Matthew 11:12)*.

# Chapter 6

# *Giessen Germany*

## The greatest gift is love

**B**ill's orders arrived before mine and he left for Germany right after Thanksgiving. We both prayed we would be together by Christmas. I was confident that Jesus would look after us every step of the way. I received my orders the week of Christmas.

The particulars and paperwork were beyond anything I had ever experienced and with it there was a new level of warfare that required deeper faith!

In order to ship my car, it had to be spotless. If it rained on my three-hour trip to the boat dock, the car would have to be cleaned again. The pressure was on in every area of my life because I was consumed with trying to meet army standards. There was no choice but to comply.

My heart was terribly grieved to be leaving the move of God at the bus garage. On the inside, I could hear myself saying over and over, "I must be smack in the middle of where God is moving." This had been my prayer since I found out we were relocating, but now the heat was on and I needed grace to endure all the emotions and warfare. "God help me!"

The departure date of December 23 arrived. My heart was grieving but my dad had some assuring last words. He said, "Don't worry, you won't stay in Germany for three years. You'll be home sooner than you think." According to army regulations, Bill had to commit to at least a three- year term overseas. Could this be a word from Father God through my earthly father?

My dad handed me a little copper coin his dad gave to him as a young man the first time he traveled overseas. There was a carved picture of an angel watching over a child. He told me he loved me and would be praying for me. My heart was tearing apart.

It had been equally difficult saying good-bye to my church family. I was 36 years old and it was the first time in my life that I had been pastored and involved in a church filled with wisdom and safety. I struggled with the fact that this rare opportunity had come to an end.

To me, Germany was death to all my dreams. Everything I believed for was dying. I prayed, "Lord, if we are not supposed to live in Germany then I break the power of every order issued to us that is not from You. You can move heaven and earth. I ask You to speak to whoever is in charge to issue Your orders. I pray this in the name of Jesus and leave it in Your hands."

A small plane took me to the larger airport where I was to catch a military charter. When I arrived, my nightmare began. My luggage didn't make it and I needed to check my bags immediately for them to be on the plane to Germany.

It was raining. I kept running back and forth between terminals to see if they had located my baggage. The other terminal was out the door, down the block, up the escalators, and down at the last gate. The man first helping me had gone home but neglected to tell anyone to follow up with my situation. By this time, I was concerned that I would be off to Germany with none of my belongings.

"Jesus could You bring someone to help me?" A man standing next to the baggage counter overheard my pleas for help. He seemed to have authority because he instantly called the airline that I had flown from in New York. They informed him that my luggage was left behind to lighten the load. Their intentions were to send my luggage out the next day not realizing Germany was my destination. The man helping me gave them an order to put it on the next available flight. There was one more flight that night, but it wouldn't make it in time for my departure. "Jesus take full control and make what is impossible to man possible this night."

Back to the other terminal I went, a bit dismayed. When I arrived I learned my flight was delayed two hours. Quickly I ran back to the other terminal to let them know I could pick up my baggage as soon as it arrived. "Thank you Lord for sending Your angels to help me."

Finally my luggage arrived, intact. While wheeling it in-between the terminals, a bus zoomed by and splashed me, causing me to startle. The baggage tipped off of the cart and into the road. I just wanted to cry. I picked everything up and prayed again, "Lord, I am confident that you will continue walking through this night with me."

The plane to Germany was delayed again until 1:30 a.m. There were 300 of us waiting to board. Mothers were without their husbands, struggling to manage their children. Only a few of us offered to help. The kids were so stressed and afraid, there wasn't much anyone could do that seemed helpful. My heart went out to them. It was far more difficult for these mothers. "Help all of us endure this night, Jesus. Not just me."

Finally at 2:00 a.m. we boarded the plane. I was exhausted and wanted to sleep. It wasn't that simple. My seat was next to a mom with her three distraught, crying and kicking children. She held her infant the entire flight. Since sleep wasn't possible, I read my Bible. The Lord and I had a very intimate conversation in the midst of the chaos. "Lord please speak to me about this move to Germany; I am so desperate." The first words I read were *Exodus 33:14* which reads, *"...My Presence will go with you, and I will give you rest."*

"Oh Lord, if You go with me, I'll go anywhere." I was identifying with Moses' earnest desire for God to go before him. "Please honor my obedience to move to Germany. Surely You can change our orders if we are not supposed to stay. It's hard to believe You would uproot us when Your Spirit was exploding at work."

Bob Jones, a prophet, had told me six months ago I was about to go through a test of faith. This was the test but I didn't realize it yet.

All through the flight the Lord conversed with me. He said He would prosper me and bring me home with many possessions. "But Lord, "I answered, "I don't want many possessions." He explained it was His desire to bless me for all the years I bypassed vacations to advance His Kingdom.

I answered, "I wasn't concerned about vacations anyway, but only to live where the revival of your Spirit dwells. You've changed me and I'm ruined. I can't have it any other way!"

At that moment, I put my hand on the child next to me and stroked her, praying for God's rest. She instantly fell asleep so there was peace for a few hours.

We landed in Frankfurt, Germany, two days before Christmas. Bill was waiting with a big smile and a beautiful rose. I told him all about the trip and we laughed. This last month alone was difficult for him too. He rode his bicycle to work everyday in full army uniform, even in the rain. Communication was confusing in his new unit. It seemed totally different from anything he trained for during the last 16 years.

When we arrived at our quarters, Bill explained overseas housing regulations. Without housing, the spouse is not allowed to join the soldier. This is why my orders had been delayed. Bill, being a little higher in rank, asked them to find him something temporary so I could join him as soon as possible.

I should have known that we would move again. According to the prophecy, there were still fourteen more months of change and transition.

Up, up, up, eight flights of stairs to this temporary apartment. It was more like a motel since it contained eight bedrooms. It used to house the cleaning personnel for the building. How interesting, God had moved us into literal *servants quarters.*

All our appliances needed adapters. We had one standard American outlet in the kitchen. That's where I could blow dry my hair. The basement was equipped with a laundry facility. Thank goodness I loved to exercise; I would certainly get a workout running down those 64 steps and back up lugging laundry. The washers didn't have automatic softener dispensers, so adding softener was another 128 steps.

I considered leaving it out, until I experienced what the water in Germany did to our clothes.

We were told our car would take a few months to arrive. That meant I would walk to all the government appointments. I Typically loved the outdoors, but here it was always raining making walking a big chore. It was the middle of winter so the rain froze making it treacherous as well. The winds blew so hard it was impossible to keep my umbrella from turning inside out. Between slipping and sliding, fierce winds and pelting rain, I had my work cut out for me just to get to my destination.

Giessin means, "to pour." It certainly fit the description of the weather here. "Lord, please bring some sunshine. Let it be a token of your desire to shine upon the people here." The same day the sun came out and stayed out for an entire week. Everywhere we went people were remarking about the change in the weather. I was thankful. For me it was a kiss from God.

The first month was extremely challenging. Bill's unit was to rotate six months in and six months out of Saudi Arabia. This would leave me in Germany, unsettled and by myself. It didn't take me too long to realize army orders were not always God's intent for us. I learned to take authority in the name of Jesus over every government order and insisted we would only receive orders from the Kingdom of God. This became an important prayer throughout our service to the military.

One night an army wife questioned me, "Don't you expect your husband to go off to all these places? After all, he is in the army and it is his duty." I explained that wherever God wanted Bill to go I would be glad. But I was not going to sit back and let the strategic plan of the enemy have its way. Our experiences were more that mere circumstance. We were in a battle with the forces of darkness. Hopefully something good was about to happen.

The paperwork was unbelievable as if I no longer had a name or a social security number. Everywhere I went, they asked me Bill's name, Bill's rank and Bill's social security number. Women were just about invisible. Bill told me there was an old army saying: "If Uncle Sam wanted you to have a wife, he would have issued you one." Just great! I was single until I was 35, and now I couldn't do anything without Bill's signature. The Lord continuously reminded me, "Keep your heart clean, Rosey. Don't entertain anger or bitterness and I will see you through this season."

Europe has a great bus system, that's assuming one can learn how to use it. I tried to obtain help from Germans waiting for the bus, but that was nearly impossible. Most people would not even look at me when I spoke to them. It was like they were deaf. In desperation I resorted to using mime to communicate

Each new day confirmed my need to learn the German language. Prayer for divine appointments for people who could communicate with us occupied my lips daily. God answered those prayers and continued answering them during our entire stay in Germany.

Why were the residents of Giessin so unfriendly? Everyone told me German people were warm and hospitable. If only I could read German, I would research the history of this city.

I brought my questions to the Army Welcoming Services and discovered some interesting information. It seemed that after the Berlin wall came down in East Germany, many refugees and poor Turkish people came to Giessin for help. Most of them were given surplus military housing to live in which caused the Germans in that area to be afraid. It wasn't the norm for them to react cold and standoffish. As we later explored other villages, we could see a big difference in how the German people extended their hands to Americans.

Also Germans have distaste for military men because of how some younger American soldiers treat the German women. This is understandable.

I further discovered that during the war, an American bomber landed on a German farmer's land. The farmer killed the American pilot with a pitchfork, piercing his entire body with hundreds of holes. When the rescue plane flew in, they found this pitiful sight. From that point on in the war, the American pilots tried to level Giessin. Every time they flew on a mission they agreed to *save a round for*

*Giessin.* As a result its historical sights were totally demolished and rebuilt in modern day architecture. This information helped explain some of the tension I sensed in the spirit.

I wanted to ride my bicycle more frequently, but the winds were so strong, at times I would literally get blown down. Walking had to do-six to eight miles a day was not unusual. I tried to pray for the houses I walked by, but truthfully it was hard. The spiritual atmosphere was oppressive; it was hard to break through alone. I had yet to find Christian support.

The commissary was four miles away. I would load an army duffel bag with groceries, heave it on my back and waddle home. I felt like a pioneer. I had to go to the German supermarkets with a dictionary to make sure I was buying the right things. A big chunk of the day was set aside for grocery shopping. After awhile it became adventurous and I enjoyed the German markets better than the commissary.

As time progressed, I figured out the bus system to the commissary. Walking a few blocks to the bus with my duffel bag seemed like a breeze. Just as I was getting the hang of this procedure, my car arrived earlier than expected. By February, I had passed my German license exam, Bill had purchased a little Volkswagen bug and I could say good-bye to those pioneering grocery days. To complete the package, I signed up for a beginning German class in hopes it would help my communication in the marketplace. It was harder than I expected.

Days were literally consumed with army paperwork. My heart grieved watching precious time get thrown out the window. Bill worked 16-hour days, came home and did paperwork until he fell asleep.

Military families experience stress overseas that civilian people don't. Loneliness, fear and depression are not unusual. Most of the women stay in the house all day. I prayed for the opportunity to tell others of God's faithfulness. When I told people how Jesus was answering our prayers, it was like pouring water on a dried up old sponge.

When I first learned that the name **Giessin** meant "to pour," it struck me in a negative sense. In the spiritual dimension it had a positive meaning. "That's what I want to do while I'm here Lord. I would like to pour out Your goodness on dry and thirsty souls. I'm relying on You to put me in the right places, and connect me with the right people."

One evening while listening to my worship tapes I had a vision. I saw myself blindfolded and tossed in the middle of a street filled with traffic. The Lord's voice was directing me, but I was afraid of getting hit. "I can't see," I said. The Lord said, "Trust me, I will not let you get hit." Right there in the chair that night, I stirred myself up and spoke words of faith to God. "Oh Lord, I refuse to let my mouth say the words I'm thinking. I can't see and I don't feel anything, but I believe You." I started shouting all around my living room, "I believe You! I believe You! I believe You!"

Bill and I followed a few leads concerning spirit-filled fellowships. Each place we visited needed an interpreter. Most of the services were in German except for one that was connected to Paul Yonggi Cho's ministry out of Korea. It was enjoyable experiencing the different cultures of the body of Christ, but we needed to find a place where we could settle in.

At work, Bill discovered that a Baptist chaplain had arrived a few months before us and started a Sunday night service. This chaplain was reported praying for a move of God in Giessin. That caught my attention. So did the fact that we arrived in Giessin around the same time. (Prior to leaving New York, we beseeched the Lord to bring laborers from all over the world to Giessin at the same time as we arrived. Could this be one of the answers?)

I decided to visit this service to see if we were supposed fellowship there. I hesitated, because some army chapels in the States were spiritually dry. They were usually kept generic so everyone would feel comfortable. On my way to the chapel I was talking to the Lord, putting in my usual request. "Lord, it's me again. Could you please put me right in the middle of Your will while we are here? Show me if this is it."

That night eight people attended. While we were worshipping the Lord spoke to me. "I am going to use you to lead worship here." They already had a worship leader, so I wondered if this could be so.

I attended the services a few times and then the worship leader disappeared. It was quite awhile before we learned his unit was called away suddenly for field maneuvers. In the interim, Chaplain Keith asked Bill and I to develop a worship service. This proved to be an interesting mix. Charismatic's leading worship for a Baptist preacher? His colleagues said this mix would never work. Were they ever in for a surprise. To my amazement, Keith told us he had been asking the Lord to send someone that would lead the people in Hosanna Integrity-type music. That was where our hearts were too.

God inspired Keith to impart a truth to our fellowship that would change us forever. We were given a divine impartation as Keith preached that the greatest gift is love.

When time allowed, Bill and I visited other German cities. I thoroughly enjoyed learning the history and culture of Germany along with the surrounding European countries. Visiting these places helped me to pray with an expanded heart for the native people. It helps to know the strongholds over an area, so you can stay alert to enemy hindrances.

Praying for myself was difficult in this season. I was going through the death of a dream and a test of faith simultaneously. My personal prayers diminished to "Lord, I believe You," over and over. Nothing bore witness with my spirit concerning our staying in Germany for three years. I knew it was completely out of my control and I could only believe that God knew exactly where I was and right where I was supposed to be.

About this time I realized I was in the middle of that test of faith that Bob Jones had prophesied. Every day I looked for something I could find to be thankful for. It was helpful to compare my needs with others; often theirs were greater.

During the hard times it's so important to cultivate a thankful heart. I was grateful for the encouraging letters from friends back home and thanked God for our little fellowship on Sunday nights on the base. It was the highlight of the whole week. The chaplain had a sincere heart for revival and led us in prayer for it every meeting. I was no longer alone in my desire for revival. Keith's excitement encouraged me so much that I prayerwalked that entire military base asking the Lord to open the hearts of the people.

One day Bill came home and informed me that his unit would be deactivating and returning to the States by August! I imagined that my friends and family could hear me shouting praise all the way across the ocean. I believe that it was God who literally changed government orders specifically for us. I wondered what God wanted to birth here in and through us during these nine months in Germany. Whatever it was, "Go for it Jesus!"

Bill had an impression as to where our permanent quarters would be for the remaining stay. He stumbled upon an empty apartment that the housing department must have overlooked. I had prayerwalked around that same building a few days before. The housing department approved it, but since they could not move us for a few months, we would need to move ourselves. In spite of the added stress, I accepted this offer.

With Bill's hours, he couldn't help me. That left me lugging our belongings down eight flights of stairs, packing them up in our little car and carrying them up six more flights in the new building. It was a tight time schedule. I had to clean the apartment to pass army specifications. Folks, you have no idea what clean is until you are under the spirit of perfectionism. The screws under the burners of the stove had to shine, floors had to be buffed, windows had to be spotless; everything in the entire apartment had to be cleaned like new. I was so exhausted one night that I sat back and cried.

Two weeks later, the rest of our furniture arrived from the States. It came the night before I took my German mid-term. To top it all off, our teacher failed to pace herself and informed us that our final exam would be a week after the mid-term. The stress never let up, but I knew that somehow God was using it to do His perfect work in me. It was so important to stay spiritually alert because much of what we encountered came from the pit of hell. If I didn't maintain the fight in the Spirit, I would have wanted to lay down and die. It was imperative to believe that I was strong IN

THE LORD AND IN THE STRENGTH OF HIS MIGHT—not my own. He was showing up to rescue me from every predicament I stepped into. It was quite impossible to take any credit.

We both sensed this new apartment was the exact location we were to live for the rest of our stay. It was huge with a maid's room and an extra bathroom upstairs. I immediately began prayerwalking the stairwells crying out for the other tenants' salvation. When no one was around, I anointed the doorways with oil and invited the Holy Spirit to inhabit this building with His presence.

Not long after we moved in I met Lucy, a woman who lived across the hall. Just after she received her orders to come and be with her husband, his unit rotated out to Saudi Arabia for six months. She was left to care for her eight-year-old son, unpack, and do the infamous paperwork all alone. We spoke frequently in the hall. I told her of the ways God had met Bill and me. I led her to Jesus and she started to attend Sunday evening services with us.

The first night, Lucy's son Robert, wanted to know what everyone was writing on our big board. I gave him my undivided attention and told him they were prayer requests. I asked Robert if there was anything he needed to ask God for. He put one finger to the side of his mouth and thought. Then he said, "I want to ask God to bring my father home soon." I wrote his request on the board. A few people thought it was inappropriate to encourage him. After all, his father was ordered to Saudi until June. They were concerned that if God didn't answer his prayer, it could shatter his faith forever. I thought just the opposite. God will answer Robert and his faith will be established forever. What a surprise when a few days later Robert's father called to say he'd be home next weekend, four months early. He told Lucy that everything seemed to come about suddenly. It was amazing how quickly God answered the requests we wrote on that prayerboard. I likened it to grocery shopping. We put the needs on the board, paid cash in prayer and then packed the answers up and took them home. Amazing! God showed up big time!

One night the Lord spoke to me, "It is harvest time." I quickly told Chaplain Keith he needed to find a baptismal. He didn't doubt for a minute. Keith got excited. He immediately located one dismantled in a closet of another chapel.

It was a blessing to work with Chaplain Keith. He had child like faith and loved the Lord. We didn't have to fast and pray for him to get the message. We didn't have to go through any formula or religious structure; he responded quickly and God honored this simplicity. After Keith obtained the baptismal, I was more encouraged than ever to keep prayerwalking. By the time it was set up and ready to go, five more people had given their lives to the Lord. Bill and I visited the new converts, and taught them the scriptures to prepare them for baptism. I have always believed that new converts should be baptized as soon as possible. God commanded it and it seems to somehow seal their faith.

"Here we go again," I thought. I was watching the Lord touch people and change their lives right before my very eyes. When one person got saved, they told their friends and more people would come to the service. There were 40 people attending our little service in just a few months. Chaplain Keith held a baptism every Sunday night before service started. I reflected back to Bus 23 when Helen and I were praying about leaving for overseas. We asked God to put us right in the middle of His work when we got to where we were going, and look what was happening. Oh Lord You are so faithful.

Those attending Sunday evenings requested that the worship time be extended. Chaplain Keith said he'd never heard of people wanting a longer service. Without hesitation, he granted their request, which gave me a more time to lead the people into the presence of the Lord. I had a beautiful opportunity to share with them what I learned during my quiet times of the depth of worship. God settled on us and filled the room with His presence as we waited before Him in silence.

I didn't dream things would come alive so quickly. Bill started a men's night for prayer and worship. I was helping

Keith counsel women and I held a new believer's Bible study to clean the fish we were catching. We assisted Keith in anyway we could.

When I was in prayer, the atmosphere seemed like the seal popping off a bottle of spiritual champagne. I called forth the fruit of any prayers that had been prayed before we arrived. When we take our feet to the street in prayer, we can proclaim God's promises and release the prayers that have been stored over the years.

Everyone living in our building was responsible to take a turn cleaning the stairway. I thought we could all pitch in and hire someone instead. We heard about a man, Waldo, who was cleaning another building.

We spoke to Waldo and he told us that he and his wife, Andrea had come to Giessin from Chile a few years ago. He had wanted to get a college degree here. Meanwhile Andrea gave birth to two children. They ran out of money, and he couldn't finish school. Now they were stranded in Germany. The only way they survived was by cleaning for Americans on the military base; the German government didn't allow them to work off it's economy. The Holy Spirit instantly touched Bill. He embraced Waldo, gave him a large sum of money and told him God would help him.

Waldo then told us that he was a born-again Christian and that there used to be a church in Giessin that was really on fire for God. He said the pastor left on government orders and it was never the same. My ears quickly perked up. It seemed so obvious in the spiritual realm that some-body had prepared the way in prayer before we arrived. We told him about the little chapel and he and his family became involved. Waldo became more than our official stairwell cleaner, he became our friend.

Waldo and his family lived in a small apartment. All four of them slept on the floor on one double mattress. They didn't have any furniture, but you never would have known it from their grateful attitudes. Their lives spoke a loud message. We learned much from watching them.

It was finally official that Bill's unit would deactivate. We were no longer concerned about him going to Saudi. I won-dered where we would be sent in the States. Bill wanted to stay in Europe and I was beginning to realize that home is wherever God says to go. No matter where it was, I wanted to be right where the Lord would have us,—or so I thought.

We live to be faithful servants for Him. There is no other reason to be alive. We were in the school of changes and transitions, learning to pass the tests, submit to God and trust Him in new ways. I reviewed the prophecy I was given about the many transitions before we had our orders for Germany. We had moved about nine times in the previous fifteen months. This Word had been right so far.

The army offered us a trip to Berchtesgaden on the border of Germany and Austria. It was much needed, especially for Bill, who had a very challenging schedule. There were several hotels available to the military and soldiers came from all over Germany to enjoy this breath-taking location. One evening, standing in the lobby of the hotel, I saw a young man from behind. I was sure it was someone from Highland, New York. I called his name and he turned around.

It was about two years earlier that this young man's name came up in our church for prayer. At that time he was in Saudi Arabia during the Gulf War, on the front lines in an army tank. The entire church prayed for his salvation and protection. I never heard if he lived or died. Now I was in Germany meeting up with him! God set this up for sure. I told him about our church praying for him and he told me his story admitting Jesus had spared his life. This was so divine!

Back in Geissen one evening, Bill and I learned a new convert needed $250 by the next day. We prayed with him and told him God was going to meet that need, pressed down shaken together and running over. I telephoned others from our fellowship and the word spread quickly. In less than fourteen hours we collected $635. It's great when God moves on the hearts of men for His little ones.

One Saturday afternoon Chaplain Keith called. "Can you come to the office? A woman walked in crying, and I can use your help in ministering to her." I respected his integrity. He walked wisely in his relationships with the opposite sex and didn't council to them alone. I quickly drove to the little chapel and we ministered to her.

Normally Keith spent Saturdays with his family, but he just happened to go to the chapel that day. Kelly told us she had been driving around asking God to help her. She had struggled with alcohol and drugs since she was 14. She looked up, saw the chapel and stopped. We led Kelly to the Lord. After she left the chapel, she told her neighbor what had happened. Her neighbor was about to go through a divorce; she came and we led her to Jesus too. Both of them were baptized in the little chapel on a Sunday night. Another divine set-up.

These two families joined our little fellowship, but they needed special attention we weren't able to provide. The fellowship raised money to send Kelly to a rehabilitation center in New York and opened our homes to her family in Geissen. Two of her children remained in Germany with their father. My neighbor Lucy and I took turns keeping them while their dad was at work. Often this included over night stays. Lucy was so beautiful. She cared for the children as if they were her own.

In the middle of the night, while feeding the smaller one, prophecy flowed out of me. I spoke hope for her future. "Shelly, you will be a mighty woman for the Lord one day. Don't worry about all the confusion you may experience in your life, God will use it for His glory." I anointed her forehead with oil and dedicated her to Jesus Christ. When morning came I was inspired to do the same for her brother Gavin. "Lord, I don't know if I will ever see this family again. Please Jesus, seal Gavin's Life to be holy unto You. Empower them both with faith to endure whatever obstacles come their way. Watch over them and lead them into a firmly rooted relationship with you."

Much to my surprise, their father gave his life to Jesus, started attending on Sunday nights and was baptized the same evening we baptized the battalion commander's wife. The army didn't show any sympathy for him as a single parent with two babies. He was sent to the field and still put to work sixteen hours a day. After his salvation he made arrangements to leave the army so he could be more avail-able to his children.

As plans progressed to close the base, the chapel pre-pared to close too. There was only one more Sunday service left. Keith had a death in his family so he turned the final service over to me. During worship, the Lord gave me some words of knowledge. My husband Bill and Scott, a new believer, prayed for those the words pertained to. Then I asked for all those who wanted the baptism of the Holy Spirit with the evidence of speaking in tongues to raise their hands. All over the little chapel hands went up. I invited the Holy Spirit to touch them and each began to speak in a new language. What a beautiful way to conclude the services in the Giessin North Chapel!

As the time came to shut down the entire unit, Waldo and Andrea wondered what they would do for income after everyone left. Slowly the cleaning jobs dropped off. Everyone from the chapel prayed for them. Suddenly an unusual opportunity came their way.

Waldo and Andrea knew some professional people who were leaving Germany and returning to Chili. These people had purchased two containers to ship both their car and belongings but decided not to ship the car. They offered the second container to Waldo and Andrea at no cost. All of their possessions were packed up and sent off to Chili for free. Their only need left was the cost of airline tickets. We collected some money but it wasn't enough. Sadly, they went through an entire year with none of their belongings and much struggling, before the German government stepped in and provided the means for their return to Chili.

Meanwhile everyone was busy packing, scrubbing our apartments to specifications, and waiting to leave. It was good-bye to the little chapel. The nine months in Germany were greater than I ever expected. I personally left with a deeper dimension of faith. All the struggles now seemed worthwhile. I was assured that no matter where we went, God's promises for me would come to pass. The battle was fierce in the heavenlies, but nothing would change what God said He would do.

Our move to Germany brought many new insights. I learned first-hand what military families experienced. It gave me a burden to pray for them that I didn't have before. Through it all, my Jesus is faithful and true. He did all He said He would do. Oh, how we humans look at our moments of pain and wonder how God could use what looks meaningless to work His purposes in our lives. In spite of whether we like what God is asking of us or not, He requires us to simply trust and obey. The rest is up to Him.

The Colonel called everyone to an information assembly on Forthood, Texas, our next home. He forewarned us that there wouldn't be enough base housing, rentals were scarce, and we would have to buy a house. I was leaving Germany with a deeper well of faith in the nature and character of God, so none of these concerns seem to affect me. Bill was one who would be sent ahead to prepare for the other soldiers' arrival. This put the two of us in a much better flying situation than when I came to Germany by myself. Thank God, we'd be together on a regular United Airlines flight, all the way to Texas.

On August 29, 1993, I sat back on the plane reflecting on the words the Lord spoke to me on my flight to Germany, "My presence will go with you and I will give you rest."

Scores of people were saved, baptized, and best of all, lives were being transformed. My heart entered a resting-place. I put full trust in the Lord to care for the new believers that I had left behind in New York as well as those that we were leaving in Germany.

Then I remembered the next thing God said. "I will prosper you and bring you home with many possessions." We obtained incredible amounts of furniture in Germany that we never sought after. There was a German *shrunk* (a kitchen hutch) left behind when we moved in our apartment that we obtained free of charge. The army surplus department held sales that furnished us with office furniture, a dining room set, two night tables and much more for less than $100.00. We were leaving with a few thousands pounds more than we had come with. It was exactly how the Lord said it would be.

As I pondered, I recalled Him saying He was going to bless me for all the years I passed up vacations to advance His kingdom. Bill and I had traveled a lot while in Germany. We toured the "Bunkers" where people hid underground during the World War II. We walked the wall of the medieval city of Rothenburg. We visited the "Corrie Ten Boom Clock Shop" in Harlem, Holland, where I was deeply touched by the Holy Spirit for the persecuted Church. How sobering to come face-to-face with the sorrow at *"Dachu,"* a Nazi concentration camp. We were privileged to walk freely through East Berlin, once surrounded by the infamous Berlin Wall.

What an opportunity to have taken our feet to just about every major city in Germany and Holland, believing God will one day bring a mighty revival to every one of those places.

Our eyes gazed upon ornate architecture and we discovered enlightening history that dated back to the first century. Everything was affordable to active army personnel and drivable. I was privileged far more then I had ever dreamed. When I reminisce I'm overwhelmed. We visited France, Poland, Holland, Italy, Switzerland, Austria, Belgium, and Germany.

Moving to Germany was the hardest move of my life, but Jesus poured forth an abundance of grace to carry us through. I grew to love Germany, and to my surprise it was difficult to say goodbye to this beautiful land.

# Chapter 7

# *American Soil*

Our flight to Dallas took 10 hours. An army bus then drove us three hours to Fort Hood. It was the end of August, and Central Texas had been in a drought all summer so the landscape was parched. In Germany everything is green. There I prayed for sunshine, in Texas I'll be praying for rain. I'll miss seeing the flower boxes on everyone's windows, no more beautiful green mountains lined with vineyards and trees. Texas is dry, brown and flat. It is a whole different world to me. I know it is going to be rough on my senses, as I loved God's colorful gardens. Lush gardens helped me identify with the many facets of His majesty. Most likely God would open up another side of Himself that I had yet to see here in brown, flat, dry Texas.

We arrived at Ft. Hood and everyone was in crisis. As a rule, the greater the population, the greater the problems. We were told that Ft. Hood was the largest U.S. army installation in the world. It may have been big, but it sure wasn't beautiful. I reminded myself that the only thing important was to be smack in the middle of where God was moving. Was he going to move here?

We were home on American soil but by no means did it feel like home yet. I say "yet" because God had a way of gripping me sooner or later to make it feel like home wherever we were. There were certainly some conveniences in America that in and of themselves welcomed us home: non-fat foods, books written in English, twenty-four hour grocery stores, and fabric softener sheets, hurrah! Funny, the crazy little things we missed.

Several army installations throughout the U.S. and overseas were closing and sending their troops to Ft. Hood. From our post in Germany alone were over a thousand soldiers. Another 2,000 came from Ft. Polk, Louisiana and there were 2,000 more expected from various installations. Imagine, relocating all these people at one time to settle in this community. Jobs were already scarce before we arrived. This influx of people stressed the facilities and services, day care, employment, and places to live. During the Gulf War, thousands of soldiers and family members departed Texas. Realtors went bankrupt from the abrupt change in population. In order to make up for some of the loss they raised rents and changed policies to protect themselves.

The army issues a "sponsor" to incoming soldiers. The sponsor is a soldier that already lives at the base, helps orient them and helps them find a place to live. We were blessed to have a helpful sponsor. He explained that the gates of Ft. Hood had two faces. The Far East gate put you right in the middle of a drug and prostitute-filled neighborhood. Soldiers were targeted in drive-by shootings and warned by the colonel to stay clear of this area. Totally in contrast, the West Side was a bedroom community of about 3,200 people, built up from Texas prairie land.

Searching for a house brought many surprises. If it wasn't one thing, it was another. There wasn't much to choose from, and a lot of what we looked at was either cricket-infested or too small. In the sponsors opinion, we wouldn't find anything decent unless we bought a house. This assumption was so common, soldiers from our unit didn't even look for rentals, and were buying houses left and right. Nevertheless, Bill and I were filled with faith and not afraid to share it with our sponsor. We were sure the Lord told us not to buy a house, so contrary to the popular reaction, we decided to wait for Him to steer us to our reserved spot.

Finally, one afternoon our sponsor took us into the city of Copperas Cove to search for housing. Bill asked him to stop at the first real estate office that caught his eye. When we walked in, the receptionist was on the phone telling a customer they didn't have any apartments available. She stressed she had a very long waiting list. A couple ahead of us, waiting in the lobby, she also discouraged from being put on the waiting list.

However the receptionist told us to take a seat while she took another call. We heard her repeating the same depressing information. I don't know why we sat there, but we did. Right after she hung up, she asked us what size apartment we were looking for. We responded and she gave us keys to two townhouses. We were stunned. I thought to myself, "This is God making a way where there is no way."

We took a peek at the townhouses and were impressed at their cleanliness. Although they were much smaller than any space we had lived in before, either could meet our needs.

The nice thing about Copperas Cove was that it was a non-achoholic county and Bill was close to work. Many soldiers had to take housing an hour away from Ft. Hood, which is incredibly difficult on one-car families. We were blessed to avoid this inconvenience.

After we moved in, I couldn't resist asking the receptionist why she concealed those apartments from others and gave them to us. She said, "When you and your husband walked in my office, I felt like I was supposed to rent to you. There was just something about the two of you that made me feel unusually good." I told her of our prayers and she told us that she too was a Christian. Imagine, in the middle of this crisis, God had his eye upon us.

Somehow it seemed all of these circumstances were arranged to test us and prepare us for something to come. The Lord was drilling us over and over to stand on what He told us. Then, without fail, He backed up His Word with His answers. It was reassuring to know we were in the apartment God Himself had chosen for us. He has a strategic place for His children to live. All we have to do is ask, wait and follow His footsteps. It pleases Him when we trust what He says even when the circumstances seem contrary.

However, I was not happy with where the army commanded us to go, nor was I certain that it was God's permanent home for us. I struggled with being subjected to army values and standards, but through it all God sustained me. I believed more each day that God would be with us every step of the way. It took some time to see His direction, but I knew it would come.

Bill went right to work, but I was starting over again and inevitably had to begin on the bottom rung. The report from most families was that jobs were limited. I knew I could get a job as school bus-driver anywhere in the country, because drivers were always in demand. When I found out Texas required written tests for all the endorsements on my license, I decided it wasn't worth the hassle. My license had motorcycle, hazardous equipment, air brakes, passenger and a commercial driver's endorsement. That meant an awful lot of tests just to meet Texas requirements. Instead, I noticed an ad for substitute teachers in a nearby district and applied for the job. The state laws didn't require more than a high school diploma. Much to my surprise, they hired me.

There were about 200 schools in the Killeen School District, so work was plentiful. I was sent all over the district, substituting for different grade levels until one day I was sent to the high school. The high school was outfitted with metal detectors and policeman patrolled the halls with drug dogs. Believe it or not, I felt like this was where I belonged. The opportunities were plentiful and I could leave a trail of prayer everyday throughout the school. I requested to substitute primarily in the high school. The gals in the sub-center said my request was unusual. Seldom did anyone want to substitute teach at the high school. It was by no means easy. Satan and I had some head-on collisions, but Jesus in me prevailed.

We attended a church at the east entrance of the city. It wasn't long before the pastor invited me to be a part of the worship team. Bill slid into an open slot as head usher. We were finding church fellowship, but it disturbed me that I wasn't seeing the movement of the Holy Spirit on my job. This gripped my heart. I needed Him to show me His purpose for us in Texas. Even if it was just for one person, that would be okay. I just needed to find out where He was moving so I could flow with Him. That morning in my devotions, the story about Philip and the Ethiopian eunuch

*(Acts 8:26-31)* stood out. Maybe I would just minister to one person while I was here.

Prayerwalking the streets close to home was a given, but it didn't seem like I was directed to anything else specifically. One afternoon while driving around, I lost my way. As I looked for something familiar, I turned the corner and noticed a school bus garage. I didn't realize that Copperas Cove owned their own school buses.

As I drove past, I couldn't believe my eyes. Jill, the woman I used to work with at my old bus-driving job in New York, was walking into the lot! I honked the horn frantically. When she saw me she was stunned. "Rose, goodness gracious," she said, "What are the chances that this could ever happen?" Tears were rolling down my face, and I said, "beyond a shadow of a doubt, this is a divine appointment. God set the whole thing up." She agreed. It was the first time she clearly acknowledged the Lord's workings to me.

Jill had met a woman soldier with orders for Ft. Hood and they moved to Texas. She had to be much more secretive about her lesbian lifestyle here than she was in New York. As a result her friendships were pretty shallow. "I have been very lonely here and in desperate need of a friend," she said. "I believe this is an act of God that you are here." I told her I got married, moved to Germany and ended up in Texas.

Jill told me they needed drivers and she could get me a job. I wasn't interested but she convinced me to meet her boss. Her boss offered me a job that had the same hours as Jill's. In fact the bus she offered me was assigned the parking slot right next to Jill's. That run even had a mid-day time slot that only a handful of drivers were offered, Jill was one of them. I don't know why, but I accepted this job. I was going to have to go and take those tests after all.

Jill and I talked a lot at work. For the first time she was open to the things of God. I tried to show her His love in all I did, without compromising the Gospel message. We had some good times together and were becoming life-long friends. Even though God was working overtime on her heart, I could tell it wasn't the hour of her salvation. She still had so many fears and misconceptions of who God was.

I'm certain His hand continues to be upon her and His mercy is slowing wooing her. I believe she will be a mighty woman in the kingdom of God one day.

It was October and I was still struggling about living in Texas. It just didn't feel right. In four more months the prophecy about 24 months of change and transition would be over. At the end of this period there was supposed to be a commissioning backed with His power. It was around this time frame that Bob Jones, a prophet of the Lord, told me that God was re-commissioning me to do something in Texas. I didn't want to be re-commissioned. In the past none of Bob's words to me ever fell to the ground, but this time I thought for sure he'd missed it.

Two months after our conversation I was driving in my car. My worship tape ended and popped out of the deck. The radio announced something about *March for Jesus*. Following a prompting in my heart, I found the names of two gentlemen coordinating the march in a nearby city. They invited me to a meeting in January and encouraged me to attend a conference in Dallas a few weeks later. They were convinced that God wanted me to lead a *March for Jesus* in Copperas Cove. I didn't feel that at all. It seemed more likely that I would jump in and help them, then to take on a whole city myself. Besides, as of yet I really didn't have a vision or a passion for the people in Texas. God would certainly have to speak to me to show me they were accurate.

I did attend the conference. No one had to convince me that the *March for Jesus* vision was valid. Many years before it was introduced into the United States, I had very similar multicolored visions of Christian praise marches. My dilemma was that in those visions, the praise marches took place in the Hudson Valley. The entire time at the conference, I kept asking God to help me. Deep inside my heart, I still believed I was supposed to bring the march to New York. With Bill's career this was impossible. The Holy Spirit was gripping me until I finally needed someone to talk to about the pushing and pulling going on inside of me. What was God trying to say?

I shared my concerns with John, a conference speaker. He prayed for God to speak to me that night and settle the issue. During worship the presence of God was really evident. Tom Pelton, the president got up to the platform and said, "I believe God wants to re-commission those of us here tonight." I was jolted. Those were Bob Jones' very words to me just a few months back. Immediately, I was humbled and asked the Lord to forgive me.

I surrendered, "Oh Lord, if this is what You are commissioning me to do, I am willing, but I have one request, would you burn a love in me for the people of Copperas Cove so I just don't go through the motions?" The fire of God instantly shot through my stomach. I wept intensely with groans too deep for words.

When the work of the Spirit was through, I got up and had a God carved passion on my heart to call the City of Copperas Cove to *March for Jesus*. I had no reputation there whatsoever. Not a soul knew anything about me and I didn't know anyone. Only God could pull this off. One thing I was confident in was that He usually does a pretty good job.

As I drove home I realized the 24 months of transitions were over almost to the day, fulfilling the prophecy given to me in New York. The rest of that word said I would see a settling of the Lord and that He would send me out with power at the end of 24 months. Part of me was excited and hopeful. Maybe we had come to the end of the transitions. It was also a blessing to be clear on what God was commissioning me to do in this season.

Still, I knew that the more clearly God speaks, the more trials there are to endure before what He has spoken comes to pass. After what just happened, I couldn't refute what my orders were. I would rely on His grace again to carry me through. It was February and I had until June to put this whole endeavor together. There was so much work to do. *March for Jesus-Copperas Cove* was on its way!

# Chapter 8

# *Taking The Bride To The City*

**W**hen I arrived home, Bill and I talked about God commissioning me to lead the city in a *March for Jesus*. Though he gave me his blessing, I was unwilling to go forward without the support of the city pastors. Unity releases permission to use our authority in a different dimension. (I will address this in the next chapter.) Over the years I learned that the real battle is not with flesh and blood, but with principalities in the dark world.

My pastor was willing to help and gave me the name of the president of the ministerial alliance. Then he said, "I believe you should meet Bishop. He is a pastor of pastors who holds a spiritual key for our city. It will have to be God though; he and his wife are people of prayer and their ministry is very large." "We'll leave it up to God,"

I responded. "He will work it out."

I telephoned the president of the alliance. He invited me to share at their next meeting. On that morning the first person to greet me was Bishop. This was a divine appointment.

I shared my heart with the pastors concerning the *March for Jesus* vision and the necessity of us all working together. I said to them, "Without pastoral support there is too much unnecessary warfare that I will encounter doing a city-wide event. If you say no, I will not move forward. I'm here to serve your heart for this city, not my own."

At that meeting I was released to oversee the most challenging job I had ever undertaken. It would produce tremendous fruit for the city and for me personally. I left with a multi-demoninational pastoral steering committee in place. I had never met any of those pastors. Only a few weeks before I had no clue I would be doing this. The Holy Spirit can show us the Father's direction in moments. I was transferred into a different realm overnight.

Several churches offered the use of their copy machines and office staff. Pastor Billy was tremendously gifted in advertisement and public relations. Pastor David encouraged me when things got rough. Garon, a church secretary helped me out of the big messes I created while learning to use a computer for the first time in my life. Bishop, and his elder, drove around the city to show me where everything was located. These and so many others opened their hearts, hands and facilities. The support was outstanding.

Even with this encouragement, I knew that a ministry could never go higher than its level of prayer and praise, combined with fasting for all the particulars. It was crucial to mobilize prayer to firm up the foundation. Prayer prepares the way for what God wants to do. It would be very presumptuous to think that we could go forth in the flesh and God would bless it. I can't stress enough that prayer must precede the work. Now that we were moving out of the church into the streets, God desired specific prayer to target this corporate celebration.

Divinely, the Holy Spirit formed a multi-denominational group that met several times a week for a 5:00 a.m. prayer meeting to pray for the *March for Jesus*. In addition, I launched prayerwalks throughout the city. Our goal was to pray for revival on every city street. Excitement stirred as some of the pastors organized prayerwalks as a part of their mid-week services.

Seventy people from various churches showed up at our first prayerwalk. We split into groups and covered nearly half the city. During the prayerwalk I listened intently to Gabriele, a woman on my team as she prayed. My friend Richard pointed out the similarity in style between the two of us. I was holding back laughter. She sounded just like me.

It was more than style though; she was praying word for word what I had prayed a few nights back. This was prophetic.

Later she told me she had been prayerwalking this city for years. Then she boldly said that my coming to town was an answer to her prayers. "I prayed you in," she said. I laughed so hard I almost cried. She was probably right. Her groundwork of prayer provided unusual favor and freedom for me in the city.

We continued pressing in with prayer even when only a handful showed up. The Bible tells us that one can chase a thousand and two can put 10,000 to flight *(Deuteronomy 32:30)*. As long as there were two or more of us, we kept right on prayerwalking.

The Lord placed it on my heart to develop a citywide prayer calendar for God to be glorified in our city. Each church was assigned a day to fast and pray prior to the *March for Jesus*. The city granted permission to hold prayer meetings at city hall as long as all the churches in the city were invited. All our prayers focused on revival and city-wide unity.

Prayer was taking place "across cultures, genders and denominations. Things were falling into place. The Holy Spirit quickened *Psalm 133* to me:

> *"Behold how good and how pleasant it is for brothers to dwell together in unity! It is like precious oil upon the head, coming down upon the beard, even Aaron's beard. Coming down upon the edge of his robes. It is like the dew of Hermon, coming down upon the mountains of Zion; for there the Lord commanded the blessing - life forever."*

This city was filled with incredible godly leadership who wanted the Lord to command the blessing. They worked together in unity to give Jesus a day of extravagant worship. It's noticeable when leaders in a city are praying and working together. The spiritual ground is so much easier to till.

Doors opened for me to share our vision on TV, radio, in newspapers and in more than 30 churches and ministry meetings. No one in this town knew me prior to this endeavor, so this was all a surprise. It happened very fast.

In the middle of the city was a witchcraft museum. Several prayerwalks were directed past this location. The March route was mapped out to take us right by it. Local pastors had witnessed to the owner. There were lots of people praying for its removal. Up to this point nothing visible had happened. We kept praying for the witches' salvation and for this business to close.

One afternoon while driving through the March route, I repeatedly commanded the Devil to loose his hold on the witchcraft museum. I was praying for the entire store to be shut down and the coven connected with it to know Christ. All of a sudden, I experienced heavy spiritual warfare. Each time I passed the witchcraft museum, a sharp pain like that of a sword, shot across my chest. It increased until I thought I was having a heart attack.

I drove myself to the army clinic a block away. The first thing I did was to grab the phone and alert the prayer chain. While the doctor monitored my heart I was reciting the Word of God and praying in the Spirit. After awhile the pain subsided and my breathing normalized. It was evident the prayer support had taken me through to the other side of the battle. From this incident I learned it was best not to pray for that place all alone. This is a key to many fatalities in the body of Christ. There are certain things we do not have permission to do alone. We need each other.

One day I found two unusual messages on my answering machine. One was from the owner of the museum wanting to advertise for us by putting our poster in his window; the other was the police department. The police department told me that the owner of the witchcraft museum was concerned that we were going to protest in front of his building when we marched.

I reassured the police that *March for Jesus* was not a protest, but an act of worship. They asked if I would visit the owner of the museum. He was very upset and asked them to change our route. Bill and I phoned the pastors' steering committee and our prayer support. I had never met the owner before, but I had seen him driving his truck around with several disgraceful bumper sticks on the back like: "Born Again Pagan," and "Death is Beautiful." We phoned him and set an appointment. Neither Bill nor I had been inside the museum before. I strongly believed we weren't to preach to him. Dozens of believers had already spoken to him throughout the years. He was well informed on how to receive Christ. We were to stand firm in the Lord.

When we arrived at the museum, the owner introduced us to his assistant. He addressed this gentleman as a high priest in the Wiccan religion. He also let us know that he and his wife were ordained Wiccan pastors in Texas. We were invited to a seat in a palm reader's booth. Darkness was swirling around me, along with a defiling presence of unholiness. I could see at the back of the museum a meeting hall where they held their masses. The front of the store was filled with religious artifacts from different cultures. This was a battle between darkness and light. The Lord kept reminding me to stay focused on Him.

It was difficult to get a word in. This man was rapidly telling us everything he believed, trying to convince us of his doctrine. He told us that there were 700 others in central Texas associated to the same coven. I thought he was exaggerating. It was obvious he was very nervous about Christians marching past the front of his store, extravagantly worshipping Jesus. That kind of news was shaking up the kingdom of darkness. What would happen when we actual marched?

We assured him we were not going to protest his museum or destroy his property. We explained that *March for Jesus* was a gift of our worship to Jesus because He is worthy—not a media stunt or a protest.

"It is not about focusing on you or any of our differences, it's about exalting the King of Kings and Lord of all Lords. We are expecting at least 2,000 participants for our first march right here in Copperas Cove," I explained. "We are joining with millions that will be marching all throughout the world the same day." He was taken back by this information. "It's just for Jesus, because we love Him and He is worthy," I said.

He was determined to get a poster for his window. He repeatedly tried to convince us that the Wiccan religion was in harmony with all religions. I spoke softly. There was a sincere burden in my heart for his soul and all those who followed him. Gently, but without compromise I said, "We are here to assure you that we are not going to destroy your property and to answer your questions concerning the poster. We can not allow you to put a poster in your window because we worship a different God. If our poster were in your window, people would think the god you served is equal to the One we serve. Satan is a god too, but he is not THE God of the universe. We did not come to convince you of what we believe, nor to hear what you believe."

I concluded by saying, "Jesus loves you. He died for all of you affiliated with this coven. There is no one that comes to Him that He would cast out. Come, give your life to Jesus and march with us; we welcome you."

With a stiff neck he said, "Oh, no thanks."

Bill and I left reminding them that Jesus was just a prayer away. My heart was terribly burdened for their souls. Could it be possible that there were 700 practicing witches right here in central Texas? I didn't believe it, but other reputable ministries that had done research in this arena said the figures were highly probable.

June 25th came. Two thousand people gathered to march. Banners were raised high as we worshipped Jesus. His presence was tangible in the air. As we marched past the museum, the owner, the high priest and others were boldly standing outside. I gave the order to stop in front of the museum while banners waved and voices exalted the King of all Kings. The presence of the Lord spilled out like fine wine. Marchers told these spectators that Jesus loved them. One marcher gave the high priest a *March for Jesus* sweatshirt. He offered her money, but she refused. Some hugged them. It was made known that we loved them, but that we were on opposite sides. We continued to march and concluded in the parking lot of the oldest Baptist church in town.

With one voice we prayed together as a city. When Bishop prayed he declared Psalms 133 over us. I secretly smiled. It was the Word of the Lord. Toward the end of the rally Alvin, an evangelist, gave a salvation call. Two young people came forward. Trailing behind them was their mother, weeping. While we were praying for the mom, she confessed her involvement in witchcraft. I believe she was a token first fruit to all the prayers prayed for the witches' salvation.

Several pastors from different denominations prayed for revival in our city. It was beautiful to see them all sharing the same platform together. Churches throughout the city reported that there was an evident difference in the level of God's presence in their services following the March. Reports came in of scores of people giving their lives to Jesus. We could sense that the King of Glory had rested His feet in Copperas Cove. All the hard work seemed worth it.

The next day a friend from Lampasses, Texas called. She was reading a local paper that said that during the same time as March For Jesus there was a recruiting rally for the KKK on the court house steps of Lampasses. It was public knowledge that Copperas Cove had a very large population of African-American Christians participating in the March, so KKK members planned to crash it. During our high praises the Holy Spirit released protection against this evil. The KKK's van suffered a blowout on their way to Copperas Cove. No one would assist them. We marched and didn't even know that God was protecting us from them. Oh, God is so good. His eye watches over the righteous and protects them. *Psalms 34:7 "The angel of the Lord encamps around those who fear Him and He rescues them."*

We continued conducting the same prayerwalks and prayer meetings into 1995. I learned that to really lay a good foundation for this kind of event, we needed full-time, year-round prayer support. Trying to pray everything together a few months before the March was less effective. Our 5:00 a.m. prayer meetings produced quick answers to our requests. Every street in Copperas Cove had been prayerwalked twice.

The very last prayerwalk before the 1995 March was different. Just a handful attended. Twelve denominations were represented; it seemed like a divinely picked team. All 12 of us prayerwalked together ending up at the witchcraft museum. The Holy Spirit prompted us to link hands and stand directly in front of the museum. There was an unusual apostolic anointing. We declared and decreed the word of God. Here are some of the things we prayed in the name of Jesus:

1. We declare that the kingdom of God be established in this building, as it is in heaven.

2. The Christians in this city are all in agreement and after today you can not stay here any longer. We evict you.

3. We decree that the souls connected with this coven will hear the glorious gospel and be our inheritance in the kingdom of God.

4. We asked that their eyes to be enlightened to the love of Christ and for truth to prevail over Satan's deception and schemes.

We concluded by proclaiming the power of the blood of the cross to the site and anointed the building and sidewalk with oil. To my surprise, the warfare following was very minimal. Reflecting on the first time I had prayed alone, I could see what the Holy Spirit was trying to teach me.

*March for Jesus* 1995 came. The route was the same. It had poured buckets of rain all night long. I woke a few times and spoke to the rain. "It's OK for you to rain now, but when 7:30 comes you will need to stop in the name of Jesus. We are having a celebration for Him and the sun must shine." Others all over the city prayed too. I got up very early to pick up the sound men and the equipment and it was still raining. They refused to set up equipment in the rain. I assured them that by the time we got to the stadium it would stop. In our early morning prayer meetings during the week, we prayed for the sound crew to be saved. It was obvious that they were not Christians. I'm sure they probably thought I was strange. They were soon to see the power behind the name of Jesus.

When we arrived at the stadium I walked around the field in the rain praying and speaking to it. I was reminding the rain that there was going to be a celebration for Jesus today and that it must stop. A short time passed and the clouds rapidly parted. The sky became clear, exposing the sun's brightness. At that point I walked over to the sound crew and said, "I believe you can set up the equipment, the rain has stopped." They looked a little stunned, but proceeded to set up. As we gathered in the Catholic Church parking lot I could see that people were coming from everywhere to march. We doubled in number from the year before. Approximately 4,000 would openly worship Jesus Christ on this beautiful day.

Mary had multiple visions of banners throughout the year, so she organized others to help her make them. The March included over 100 banners of extravagant colors waving in the air that day, glorifying the person of Jesus as Bridegroom and King. At the head of the procession marched our pastors and the mayor. Yes! The mayor had joined us. Pastors from different denominations, both male and female, walking side-by-side linked together in heart. They were doing more than just walking together; they were openly displaying the relationships that they had worked on for many years.

Next was a beautiful, gold-painted model of the Ark of the Covenant. An unusual presence of glory filled the air. People were crying while holding each other and asking forgiveness for denominational and racial prejudices. John the youth Pastor of a Baptist church, walked over to me while being deeply touched by the Holy Spirit. Tears were rolling down his face as he said, "Sister Rose, I really love you even though we are not in the same denomination. Today with all my heart, you are my sister." We wept together in the midst of thousands of people. We took the Bride of Christ to the city of Copperas Cove for all to see. It was true and holy. God was really there. The Holy Spirit was honoring our efforts to walk together and was empowering us with unity as a city of believers.

*John 13:35 "By this all men will know that you are My disciples, if you have love for one another."*

There were more spectators than the year before. People were on their porches and in their yards waiting to see the celebration. Not one was passed by without being spoken to. Many of them were interviewed by our mobile video crew and gave touching responses.

Then we came to the witchcraft museum. This time, no one was outside. In the window hung a sign that said, CLOSED FOR THE DAY. The marchers roared in victory. I knew it was closed forever!

This time the March ended in the high school football stadium, which had been closed to religious organizations for 20 years. No other religious groups had been permitted to use it. God opened the doors wide for our prayer rally to be held there. As the altar call was made, more people came to receive Jesus than the previous year.

I noticed the owner of the sound company walking across the field. Was he trying to adjust something? No, he was coming forward to receive Christ. As I witnessed his salvation I was brought to tears. Pastor Ed held him like a dad. It was a marvelous sight.

A week later, I drove past the museum and noticed a big sign in the window, GOING OUT OF BUSINESS, 50% OFF EVERYTHING. I nearly drove over the sidewalk rejoicing, shouting and praising God. "Yes! Yes! Yes! You must go!" One week later, I went back again to take a picture only to find a completely empty building. I got out and prayed for the Lord to fill that old building with His presence. (Today another business fills that place).

Scores of people prayed for years for this museum to close. How did we get the victory? I believe we were given permission to use our authority the night twelve representatives were present on the prayerwalk. We prayed across denominations in unity, took our *FEET TO THE STREET*, and God commanded His blessing.

When the devil saw the whole city in unity against him, he had to flee. I wholeheartedly believe that is when God commanded the blessing. The authority was always present in us by the indwelling Holy Spirit, but there was a moment we were waiting for so God could grant the permission for us to use it. When the moment came, we were prepared. And after we had exercised our authority, we knew *Copperas Cove would never be the same.* Let's look at this subject concerning the difference between having all the authority as a believer but not always having the permission to use it.

# Chapter 9

# *Authority Versus Permission*

This chapter addresses an important issue concerning the believer's authority. I do not go into great detail, but merely share some wisdom and precautions.

I believe that we have all the authority we will ever need, but we don't always have God's permission to use it. We need to discern God's ways concerning His authority.

In chapter four I discussed how we are the temple of the living God. Hopefully we understand that everything we will ever need is present in us through the power of the Holy Spirit. All the gifts of the Spirit, all the authority we need to operate those gifts and all the power to subdue the works of darkness are given to us when we receive the Holy Spirit. However, we are not given permission to use this authority apart from a close fellowship with Jesus. It's our Daddy's desire for us to be fruitful. He wants us to subdue the earth and rule over every living thing. I spoke about how much God likes us and desires to do His Kingdom work through friendship with us. He can do anything without us, but because of His covenant with mankind, He will not. It should be our quest to learn to cooperate with Him in everything we do. Apart from Him, we can do nothing.

In the Websters New World Dictionary ©1980, authority is defined as, *"The power or right to give commands, enforce obedience, take action, or make final decisions; jurisdiction."*

Let's see how close the dictionary is to the actual Greek meaning of authority taken from Strong's Concordance:

> *Exousia (1849) (ex-oo-see'-ah);* (in the sense of ability); privilege, i.e. (subjectively) force, capacity, competency, freedom, or (objectively) mastery (concretely, magistrate, superhuman, potentate, token of control), delegated influence: KJV—authority, jurisdiction, liberty, power, right, strength.      *(Biblesoft Version 2 ©1992-1995)*

*Matthew 10:1* states:

> *"And having summoned His twelve disciples, He gave them authority over unclean spirits, to cast them out, and to heal every kind of disease and sickness."*

We see that the disciples were given the power to evict demonic forces. In *Matthew 28:19*, Jesus commissioned His disciples to go and make more disciples and to teach these new disciples the same things Jesus taught them. Are you a disciple? If you are, then the same authority has been given to you.

Here are a few more scriptures so you know this concept is biblical.

Jesus is speaking to His disciples in *Luke 10:19*,

> *"Behold I have given you authority to tread upon serpents and scorpions, and over all the power of the enemy, and nothing shall injure you."*

Notice *Mark 16:17-18*,

> *"And these signs will accompany those who have believed: in my name they will cast out demons, they will speak with new tongues; they will pick up serpents, and if they drink any deadly poison, it shall not harm them; they will lay hands on the sick, and they will recover."*

*John 14:12-17* states:

> *"Truly, truly, I say to you, he who believes in Me, the works that I do shall he do also; and greater*

*works than these shall he do; because I go to the Father. And whatever you ask in My name, that will I do, that the Father may be glorified in the Son. If you ask me anything in My name, I will do it. If you love Me, you will keep my commandments. And I will ask the Father and He will give you another Helper, that He may be with you forever; that is the Spirit of Truth, whom the world cannot receive, because it does not behold Him or know Him, but you know Him because He abides with you, and will be in you.*

Authority is given to disciples who have the Holy Spirit living inside of them. A disciple is a born-again believer, walking in a love covenant with Jesus Christ, desiring to be obedient to God's Word and ways. Here is a scripture to ponder:

*"Now to Him who is able to do exceeding abundantly beyond all that we ask or think, according to the power that works within us."*

*Ephesians 3:20*

When we became born-again and filled with the Holy Spirit, we were given power over the enemy. Although we have this power and authority, God has set a divine order as to when and how we are to use it. It is not like authority we experience in the world, it's divine authority. That means we can only use it in conjunction with what the Father is doing. God will extend His power according to the measure of faith, obedience and friendship we operate in, with Him, through His Word. I want to reemphasize that we believers have all the authority we will ever need, but we don't always have the permission to use it. Unfortunately, there are circumstances when we do have the permission and still allow the enemy to walk all over us.

God created Adam and Eve in His own image. In the first chapter of Genesis, God told them to *subdue the earth* and to *rule over all the fish in the sea, all the birds in the sky and over every living thing that moves on the earth.* Mankind had the power and right to give commands, enforce obedience, make final decisions and take jurisdiction over every living thing. Mankind's original state was to be subjected to God only. That tells me the spiritual image that God created us in was lost after the fall. In *Luke 19:10,* Jesus states *"For the Son of man is come to seek and to save that which was lost" (KJV).* Notice He does not say, *"he who was lost."* Jesus says, *"that which was lost."* Jesus fully restored His image in us through the cross and resurrection. It's up to us to release what has been restored in us when we became born-again. He has put us in charge and we need to stand up and take the Kingdom back by force, BUT NOT WITHOUT HIM!

When I first began to exercise my authority as a believer, I was clueless that God had a divine order. It took some hard lessons to realize that I could only do what I saw the Father doing. Several times I was emotionally devastated by spiritual warfare. Twice I was physically injured. I eventually realized that knowing God's word and His ways was imperative for my protection. It is essential to see where He is working and where He is not. Don't feel condemned when you make a mistake. Run to the Lord, He will help you. Independence had to be ruthlessly dealt with in me so I could develop a closer working relationship with the Father. I'm thankful that the Lord never let go of me during those early times. Hopefully, I can help others avoid the pitfalls I fell into.

Going to war in the spiritual realm requires that we abide in God's Word. We especially learn to wait on Him for the permission to go left or right. We must know Him if we want to establish His purposes on the earth. Now, as I've grown a bit wiser, I am not as hasty. From time to time my flesh wants to run ahead. The fear of the Lord is teaching me to wait and bring my flesh under the Lordship of Jesus Christ. Husbands and wives, waiting for one another to see eye-to-eye in a matter is God's way of protecting us from moving out without His perfect timing. Adhering to each other's warnings, even when they don't seem applicable is vital. Body of Christ, there will be times to submit to leadership, even when you may not see it their way.

Having authority and the permission to use it can be illustrated through the experience I had in Copperas Cove, Texas. God gave me authority as a believer to overcome all the enemy's power. He then commissioned me to a task. Part of the permission to walk in my authority was granted when the pastors of the city gave me their blessing. God's timing allowed me to find favor with the pastors. Would I still have had the divinely imparted authority if they hadn't blessed me? Of course, but without their blessing I would have been working out from under God's canopy of protection in that city.

As we began the prayerwalks, I realized that all the pastors of the city were in agreement concerning the closing of that witchcraft museum. Because of this agreement, I asked God for His moment. It's in God's moment that He releases the power behind the authority. The moment of permission to use our authority came when representatives from 12 denominations showed up to prayerwalk. Having that kind of divine unity was powerful. That was my cue from God to give the command for the museum to close. At that moment a heavenly apostolic anointing to evict that spiritual stronghold from our city was given.

I said these very words; "We are all in agreement in this city, so in the name of Jesus I command you to go!" Just a few weeks later the building was empty. God gave the permission and commanded the blessing where brethren dwelt in unity. He made Himself strong on our behalf! Why?

The Bible tells us we can ask anything according to God's will (Word) and He will give it to us. Permission comes when we are abiding in His Word and His ways, waiting for the exact moment that He ordains. We must find out His will, support it, and then wait for His moment. Then POW!

Often I have come across Christians who refuse to pray against the enemy. They tell me that they don't have the authority. That is not the Word of truth. God's Word says that we have all the authority we will ever need on planet earth to do the work of the Kingdom. It is important to speak correctly; otherwise we are giving the dominion of darkness authority over us. So then it is more accurate to say, "I refuse to excersize my authority without God's permission."

Using our authority correctly comes from a relationship with Jesus. We are all on a quest to increase intimacy with Him. If He is not in it, then we have no business in it either. Jesus Himself said that He only did what He saw the Father doing. He had to be in close relationship with the Father in order to see what He was doing. We are to follow Jesus. That means we can learn to hear, see, and wait for the Father, like Jesus did. If the Father was casting out demons from one man, then Jesus exercised His authority toward that one man. If the Father was calming the storm, Jesus exercised His authority toward the storm.

Let's look at an account in Acts 16, Paul and Silas were in Philippi. A woman possessed with a spirit of divination was following them. She made lots of money for her bosses by predicting the future. For many days she shouted out telling everyone that Paul and Silas were servants of the most high God. Why didn't Paul or Silas immediately cast out this demon? I believe they were waiting on the Father for permission. When they cast the spirit out, "it troubled the city." A large number of people were enraged. For so many to be this affected, it had to be a stronghold over the city not just in the woman. There will be counter attacks so prepare! Paul and Silas were beaten and greatly persecuted but ended up victorious. It pays to do what the Father is doing at the right time, no matter what the cost may be.

Each different situation God calls us into requires that we walk in different levels of permission. The higher the office, the greater the responsibility to wait on the Lord for more specific details.

Sometimes it's not us God wants to use. He doesn't take away our authority, He asks us to step aside.

Another area that requires caution and wisdom is coming against a spiritual stronghold that is still an issue in your life. For example, If I tried to take authority over the spirit of condemnation in someone while it was a stronghold in my life, there would probably be a devastating counter attack of condemnation against me. I would not succeed in helping the other person either. In this case, it's better for me not to exercise my authority over that spirit. Because, when I begin to use my authority, I am declaring war. If the same spirit is in me, I can get severely wounded in the battle and wound others. It would be wiser to ask God to send His healing love into their need for acceptance and approval.

I have a little saying that I live by, "You can't give away something that you don't have." If I'm broke and someone wants to borrow $10, I can't give it to them. I can ask the Lord to give me $10 or to supply that person's need, but I can't give them what I don't have. This principle is the same when casting out demons or confronting territorial spirits. If we are not delivered from a spirit, it is not wise to try to command that spirit to leave our neighborhood. We should go to God and ask Him to free us from the stronghold. Then when He shows us the pathway out, we can exercise our authority to free others. Until then, simply ask God to satisfy their mouths with good things.

Remember that we must be in it for the long haul. It can be a long process before all the high places are pulled down in our own lives. This should not stop us from praying for neighbors and friends. On the contrary it should help us identify with their struggles, and pray more humbly. There are many scriptural proclamations we can pray over our streets without entering into illegal warfare.

If I were not free of a spirit of poverty, my prayer would be something like this,

> "Lord, You know I'm not even free from poverty, so I don't have anything to give, but You do and You can deliver us and cause us to learn your ways so that we never have to live under this spirit's domain again. Reveal your word here in my neighborhood concerning finances, so we might be able to line up with You. Brood over us and open our eyes to Your truth that sets us free. Set me free so I can be used to victoriously battle this wickedness. Show me where I am deceived or disobedient to Your ways. Show me great and mighty things I

> do not know. Let Your kingdom come and let
> Your will be done."

Don't try confronting a demon power that you have not defeated personally. Trust God! When your own freedom comes in this area, God will give you the go-ahead to tell that demon and his friends to go.

I would like to give a word of caution concerning principalities over a city. God does not give one person the permission to single-handedly call down a network of spiritual powers. Spiritual powers work in unity, without breaking ranks as a network over a city. That is how we must function to take away their jurisdiction. Because city-wide unity is scarce, this leaves most of us out. God is certainly working on the body of Christ to bring it into unity and some cities are further along than others are. Until your city is working as a network of believers in agreement and without breaking ranks, you do not have the permission to command ruling spirits and their entire networks to go. Does that mean those churches have to be completely whole? Of course not, just in unity concerning the target.

*Psalms 91:13 says, "You shall tread upon the lion and the adder, the young lion and the dragon you will trample under feet."*

Only fools rush into the enemies camp unarmed and unprepared. Let's be encouraged that God is all knowing. If we are willing to follow His ways, we will partner with Him in His blessings. He has given us the authority, and He certainly will give us the permission to use it in His time.

# Chapter 10

# *Oh NO! Transition Again?*

S urges of the Lord's glory were upon us. Signs of a real move of God were rolling into Copperas Cove. My heart was beginning to knit with the people. There was a deep appreciation in my heart for the pastors; they honored one another and that impressed me. Copperas Cove was beginning to feel like home. Much to my surprise, God had other plans for Bill and me.

At the end of December 1994, I became impregnated with something new in my spirit. I knew that the birthing time would be nine months, just like birthing a human baby. This meant around August or September of 1995 it would come into view. I was concerned that the military would uproot us again and take us away from this wonderful move of God. All my prayers were for us to receive heavenly orders, not government orders.

Bill still had two and a half years remaining in the service, with no desire to retire, or so I thought. I didn't know the Lord had begun moving on Bill's heart to retire early. He mentioned it, but I didn't take it seriously since he had always been determined to stick it out for 20 years. Unbeknownst to me, an opportunity for him to retire was offered and he passed it up. He became concerned he had missed the Lord so asked God to bring another opportunity if it was really His plan. A second opportunity would be rare for his job description, yet several months later, he was offered a better package! For Bill to accept this offer, it had to be straight from the throne room of the King. I had long since let go of any expectation of early retirement and I was taken by surprise.

The busy season for the next *March for Jesus* was quickly approaching and Bill was notified that he would retire on May 1,1995. Bill said he felt like we were going to be moving. Part of me was no longer interested in moving. We finally found a good church and 40 to 60 people were getting saved each month. The doors opened for me to attend a Bible school, something I had always desired. Things seemed to be going well. But there was that familiar stirring of the Holy Spirit. We finally asked, "If we are moving, where would You have us go?"

Months went by. I prayed for God to send me an assistant for the ministry. If we were leaving I needed the Lord to bring someone to take my place. The march drew near and no one had come forward. There was a woman I felt was the one, but she gave no indication of volunteering. Could our timing be off? Maybe we'd be around for another year after all.

I planned to go to a conference in Kansas City, Missouri after the March, then on to New York to spend time with the Lord and my family. Bill decided to come also, but wanted to go straight to New York. Kansas City was cut out. After organizing the March and prayer ministry throughout the year, this trip was well needed. We drove to New York together and arrived June 9th. We continued asking the Lord to show us where He was leading us. Was New York the move we sensed?

The rolling hills and trees were a big switch from Texas. New York was truly beautiful. For two weeks, I spent most of my time alone by the river or in the woods. The Lord brought refreshment to me. It had been quite awhile since I had such a glorious time with Him. Since leaving the Hudson Valley, I had not found this kind of outdoor seclusion.

God's tangible presence settled on me each day bringing melodies to my heart, which I sang back to Him. It seemed as though the Lord was inspiring me to keep these songs, so I sang them into a tape recorder.

Between the prayer time and the songs, I was receiving a clear message. He showed me there would be a real move of God in the next place He was sending us. Refreshment filled my soul and I felt peace. Even though we would be leaving something wonderful, it seemed we were heading toward something that we wouldn't want to miss.

During our stay in New York there were lots of interesting divine appointments. One was with my friend Helen whom I introduced to Jesus during the school bus revival that occurred before Bill and I moved to Germany. She moved to Iceland. The last time we visited New York both of us were astonished to meet up with the other. We thought that was as divinely orchestrated as it could get. This time, a year later as Bill and I were driving to New York, I said, "Wouldn't it be wild if Helen is in from Iceland again?" Sunday came and we went to our home church. A flash came across the room. Helen! Embracing each other, we cried, wondering what could God's purpose be for this wonderful meeting from different sides of the earth. Maybe Bill and I would visit Iceland one day?

Although it was always a blessing to be in New York, I realized that moving back now wasn't on God's agenda. I was persistent in asking the Lord where He was moving us. A few days before we headed back to Texas, He answered in a dream. It was a clear invitation to a church in Grandview, Missouri, a suburb of Kansas City. Who besides Mike and Diane Bickle (then senior pastors of what is now known as Metro Christian Fellowship) would give us any reason to move there?

I met the Bickles in July of 1988 by an unmistakable divine appointment. I managed to keep in contact with them for seven and a half years because of a unique connection that was made in our spirits. I pondered the dream in my heart telling no one, not even Bill. I needed some time to sort through this by myself. There were many reasons why I would not want to act on this invitation. Yet, the dream was clear enough for us to pack up and move right then. Before I said anything I waited to see if Bill would receive something to confirm it.

After three weeks we headed back to Texas. I was leaving with quite a bit to think about: a dream, four new songs, confirmation that God was not leading us back to New York right now, and the ever-present concerns for the ministry in Texas.

When we arrived in Copperas Cove, Bill looked for employment. There was very little to choose from in his field, and it was suggested that he consider relocating. Interviews were offered in several major Texas cities. We continued to cry out to God for confirmation concerning this move. The manifest presence of the Lord was still settling on me. It was an unusually sweet season. The Lord gave me visions about our future that culminated in songs. All of them brought a deep assurance to me that Grandview, Missouri was where God was taking us and that He was going to break a mighty dam and let the river flow in that city.

In the beginning of August, two months after my dream, I thought it was time to tell Bill about it. His first reaction was, "Missouri? What's in Missouri?" I didn't say a lot because I didn't think there was much in Missouri myself. Even when you think you really understand the meaning of a prophetic dream, it usually has a different way of coming about. Although I had the dream, three months of songs, visions and the manifest presence of God settling on me, Bill was not in favor of moving to Missouri. His resistance was a bit confusing. I wondered if I was misinterpreting these signs.

Then something very significant happened. We were driving to see friends in Dallas. On our way we came across a road sign that read, *"Next exit Grandview and May Pearl."* I said, "Bill did you see that? That's the name of the city in Missouri." He said, "Yes, I know that and don't get any ideas about moving there." We flew by the sign and didn't catch the numbers on it. Somehow I sensed they were significant. To me "Next Exit Grandview," was a confirmation of everything. It meant that Grandview was the next place God was going to significantly visit. He was inviting us to go there and be participants.

Waiting for each other is a key. If the partner that God spoke to doesn't wait for the other partner to hear, God's timing is often missed and the marriage suffers.

Our friends in Dallas used to be on staff at Mike Bickle's church and had just moved. They informed us Mike was going to speak at a conference in Dallas at the end of August. Interesting timing—the same time to birth what I was impregnated with nine months earlier. I decided to attend the conference. On my way there, I looked for that exit sign to write down what it said: *"Next Exit Grandview and May Pearl. Exit 15-Route 916."* I sensed these numbers were dates of some sort. So many thoughts rolled around in my head. It was beginning to sink in that we really were on our way to Grandview, Missouri—sooner or later. But more than that, I was to help them prepare the way of the Lord. He was surely going to visit there in some significant way.

I met an old acquaintance at the conference. When I told her I felt like my water was about to break in the spirit, she laughed and laughed. After nine months it was finally birthing time. Not too much was moving me on the outside during the conference, but there was a whole lot of kicking going on inside.

When Mike Bickle spoke, I saw myself washing his feet in a vision. God confirmed to me that we would soon be serving Mike's ministry.

The last day of the conference I went into deep travail, birthing what I had carried. During this intimate moment Jesus walked up to me in an open vision handing me a scroll rolled up and tied with a gold string. Then He spoke these words to me: "Here are your blueprints, your new orders." He assured me that the new order coming for the body of Christ was neither male nor female. The rest I pondered in my heart.

A month later Mike Bickle did another conference in Dallas that I also attended. By this time Bill was ready to take a trip to Grandview to see what was going on, but he was concerned that it would be expensive. Back in 1988 when I first met Mike and Diane Bickle, I prayed for the provision to visit their church in Grandview Missouri. A couple approached me saying that the Lord told them He

111

was sending me somewhere and they were to pay for my flight. I was convinced that God would provide the means again. I simply ask Him to explode with provision if he was guiding us.

Before long, friends found a $99 round trip airfare. They also gave us the number to a Kansas City realtor. When we called Barbara, she offered to help us look for houses and extended her home to us free of charge for four days. She wasn't even going to be home the first day we arrived. It sounded to me like God was on the move. A few nights later, our friends Bill and Meg said they wanted to sow into our trip and paid our airfare. I reflected back on my trip in 1988 to Grandview and said, "Ditto."

I was excited, but I could feel the fear of the Lord upon me also. This left only one more need, a rental car. Three days before we were to catch our plane, Barbara called to say she had a car we could use when we arrived. Plane tickets and a place to stay! That is how the military provides for you during a move. These were orders from heaven, and unlike the military, they even included a car. How could we doubt the answer would be anything but "Yes" for a move to Missouri?

The night before we left Texas, I had a dream that we were going to buy a house in Missouri. That was peculiar to me because Bill was more inclined to want a house than I was. In the dream I said, "Bill, that's the house we are going to live in. See, there's no one living behind us. It's an open field in back."

When we arrived in Kansas City, we spent the first day looking at apartments. The second day we looked at houses with Barbara. The next day was Sunday. We arrived at Metro Christian Fellowship for their Sunday morning service. After all, we were only moving here to attend this church and give of ourselves to prepare for revival.

Privately, Bill asked, "Lord, if this is You, would You play my favorite worship song this morning?" Bill had no idea what kind of music they played, but he knew God could answer.

When we walked in the sanctuary, the first service had ended and the second was beginning. As the worship leader began the first song, Bill's favorite, Bill broke into tears. God was going to great lengths to assure us these were His heavenly orders.

The next day I accompanied Bill job hunting. At the first interview, I sat in the car for over an hour. When Bill returned to the car, I jokingly said, "Honey, why didn't you tell me you were going to start work today? I would have stayed home!" We laughed. He was to call back at 4:00 p.m. to find out whether he was hired. There were several other places we went that morning, but they all had Bill fill out applications and said they would call him.

We looked for jobs until 3:00 p.m., then met with a loan officer about qualifying for a house. She asked Bill many questions. When she asked where he was employed, we both looked at each other.

Bill glanced at his watch; it was 3:55. He asked, "Can I please use your phone before I answer?" The supervisor answered the phone and said, "You're hired. When can you start?" Wow, what provision! Bill got the first job he interviewed for and was to start in two weeks. He hung up the phone and wrote the place of his new employment on the application.

The loan officer had a hard time believing we were telling her the truth. Right after we left, she got on the phone and called Bill's new employer to get a faxed, signed statement that he really hired Bill.

We were thankful that everything was moving smoothly. We still had a lot to do. The next day Barbara took us house hunting. Bill had a list of houses to see. Our flight left at 4:00 p.m. Barbara had us literally dashing from house to house. I was more interested in listening to the Holy Spirit than I was in the cosmetics of the houses. We were moving so fast that I had to trust the Lord would wave a big flag at us when we got to the right place.

There were a few things Bill and I asked of the Lord. One of them was that we would live in an interracial neighborhood. We left that in the hands of God and never mentioned it to Barbara.

None of the houses felt right. As we were driving, Bill noticed a few houses for sale. Time was running really short, but we insisted on seeing them. Quickly Barbara took us through the last home. "Oh, I wish we could stay here just a little longer," I said. "There's something about this house." Barbara said we wouldn't be able to stay.

We headed for the car only to find Barbara had locked her keys inside. She was certain she had another key somewhere. While Bill and Barbara searched for the spare, I slipped back into the house and prayed. The cosmetics were no different than most of the other houses, but there was a significant drawing of the Holy Spirit. Bill and Barbara returned and said we needed to wait for someone to come with a key. My spiritual antenna was up. This gave us another half-hour to look around and pray. Bill was in the kitchen looking out the window and noticed a large back yard. He liked it because there weren't any houses behind us—just a big open field. When we had enough time to look at everything, Barbara found her keys. We told her not to feel bad; God had locked her keys in the car.

Bill and I agreed to bid on this house, feeling that it could be a divine location for us. (I'm a firm believer that there is a strategic place for each of us to live. If we are faithful to ask and trust, He will show us where it is). Barbara coached us through the paperwork. It was now totally up to God to explode with His provision again.

Exhausted, we rushed to the airport. Bill and I both fell asleep on the plane. The Holy Spirit brought to my attention the dream I had before we came to Missouri. I shot up in my seat and shook Bill. "Honey, do you remember the dream I had with the big open field behind the house?"

"Yes, I remember," Bill said.

"Well, I didn't see the house in that dream. It was like we were looking out a window and could see the field. That's the house honey. That's the house." We both fell sound asleep again.

Early the next morning the phone rang. It was Barbara saying the owners had already called her back with a counter-offer. Bill told her he needed until noon. He wanted us to ask God what a fair price would be. He was strongly touched by the Holy Spirit, a figure repeatedly popped into his mind, and we believed this was our counter-offer. Barbara submitted the offer and it was accepted on the spot.

Everything was happening fast. A notice from the army arrived stating that we had 30 days to submit paperwork for a free government move. I filled out the infamous army paperwork, this time with glee, to make the moving arrangements to Kansas City, Missouri. Bill reported for his job in Kansas City and we were approved for a VA loan in less than a month. Our total house payment was $15 more per month than our rent in Texas, and the previous owners were paying every cent of the closing costs. Go God go!

All the prayerwalks, the citywide prayer, the *March for Jesus*—everything I was doing in Texas, I decided to lay down at the feet of Jesus. I was going to Kansas City emptied of any agenda, to be ready for the new thing God was about to do. The only thing I was sure of was that I would be involved somehow in preparing the way of the Lord. How and what this would look like was yet to unfold. This would be an interesting move. I had finals at the Bible school in Texas and needed to help the new *March for Jesus* coordinator. (The woman I believed would be my replacement had finally come forward). I had to pack everything up without Bill's help. This time, all the stress and physical work seemed very worthwhile. We weren't on army orders, but orders straight from the King.

Kansas City, here we come!

# Chapter 11

# *Next Exit Grandview*

We were privileged to meet the prior owners of our new home and witness God's faithfulness to them. When they asked what brought us to Kansas City I told them the whole story. Ruth, the wife, said she wondered what was wrong with her little house because it had been for sale since June with no interested buyers. I told her June was the month that I had an unanticipated dream clearly inviting us to move here. "Imagine Ruth, God held this house until November just for us. That's why it was as if no one was interested." We were both flabbergasted. Once again we are living in a divine spot.

After the house was put in order it was time for me to search for a job. I wanted a change. I interviewed for several positions for which I was qualified, but wasn't hired. Bill was certain I would drive a school bus again. I asked the Lord to allow me a vocational change, but I should have known, He had other plans.

Each time we went to church, we passed a large school bus parking lot. A big sign advertising for drivers jumped out at me. Bill was convinced that this was where my next job was going to be. I wouldn't even inquire. A month of interviews provided lots of promises, but no job.

I finally gave in to the advertisement for school bus drivers, filled out an application and was hired on the spot. What was so significant about driving a bus again and why this particular lot?

My questions were answered quickly. Heather, a Christian girl, was the regular aide for the bus I was assigned to. She had been diligently praying for a Christian driver. "So you're the one who prayed me off those receptionist jobs," I remarked. "God has plans for you and I, Heather. I could feel your prayers every time I drove past this place."

Each morning before work we would ask the Lord to visit our bus lot and to bring other Christian drivers. We would need an increase of laborers to have an impact here.

At home I prayerwalked the streets of my neighborhood. The oppression was much heavier than in Texas. It was obvious we were under a different network of spiritual strongholds here in Kansas City. What were they and how did they get here? I had some insight but it often takes years for clear discernment.

There was one significant clue, the two liberty bells and the two keys the Lord handed me in a vision, as we were moving. The keys were gold and large as if they went to a castle door. One key was gender reconciliation and the other was racial reconciliation. Were they the keys that were needed to unlock spiritual doors for a breakthrough in this city? I was unaware of any ministries holding prayerwalks or doing spiritual mapping, nor did I have a leading to start them for the corporate body. I nailed it all to the cross before I moved. This didn't stop me from prayerwalking and researching in my own private sphere. Intercession is my primary call and I try to put it to work in its many facets wherever I live. But Kansas City was different. The first thing I noticed was the slogan on the Missouri license plates, "Show-Me State." That seemed a bit arrogant. When I looked up its origin it helped me to understand the spiritual realm we were living under. The "show-Me State" originated from a speech given in 1899 by Willard Duncan Vandiver, a Missouri congressman. During his speech in Philadelphia he stated: "Frothy eloquence neither convinces nor satisfies me. I am from Missouri and you have got to show me."

The first thoughts that rang in my ears were the words, "faithless and unbelieving generation." "Oh Lord, you couldn't do any miracles where the people didn't have faith." This slogan is a curse being reinforced every day on every Missouri license plate. We can pray until the cows come home, but without faith it's impossible to please God *(Hebrews 11:6)* or to see His miracles. God should not have to show us any more than He already has. This slogan is an assault on the desire of God to raise up a family of believers that believes Him at His Word even when they cannot see.

A month after Heather and I prayed, a group of Bible seminary students were hired as drivers. The Holy Spirit inspired me to start a prayer meeting. Five of us gathered in a bus once a week, before our runs. We faithfully prayed for revival at our job-site. Although our various schedules didn't allow us to gather daily, we were praying individually. Immediately, I noticed a difference in the freedom to share Jesus with other employees. We discovered our supervisor was a Christian also. Daily the Holy Spirit stirred up Jesus conversations. When others found out we were praying, they shared their requests with us.

I was targeting a group of six fellow workers. My prayer was that the Holy Spirit would stir up questions of eternity in their hearts. About two months into our weekly prayer time, all six of them gave their lives to Jesus. One was a prodigal returning home. I spent quality time teaching them scriptures concerning baptism. One afternoon I took them to a near-by lake to baptize them. There is nothing more beautiful than to walk a person out of the kingdom of darkness and into the kingdom of light.

Things changed rapidly at the end of the school year. I sensed my mission at this job was coming to a close. When I was sure that this was the heart of God, I changed jobs. In August 1996 Bill and I were hired by the Grandview school district to work in their transportation department-Bill as mechanic and of course, me as school bus driver. For some reason I couldn't shake this job description. I was assigned to bus No.11. It looked exactly like the bus No.23 that I drove in New York.

Bus No.11 was the oldest bus on the Grandview lot and had the worst visibility, but the number was very significant to me. The first thought that came to mind was that we were walking into the *eleventh hour of the church* and the visibility is poor. God's up to something.

As usual, I spit shined that bus with Armor-All. It looked pretty good for an old clinker. Next I prayed and anointed it with oil to claim the souls of the children who would ride in it. Bus No.11 was ready to roll. I would be driving young children removed from their families by the state. In essence, they were orphans. Their needs were heartbreaking.

In November, Bill and I decided to go through the screening required to take two of the boys on Sundays. I discovered Robert, the tiny eight-year-old had never heard about God or Jesus. He didn't know Christmas was Jesus' birthday and he had never heard of prayer. Sunday after Sunday I read Bible stories to him and talked to him about Jesus. His little eyes lit up and he asked me over and over if the stories were true. He sat in church and listened to the worship intently, then fell asleep curled up next to me during the sermon. The entire time he was sleeping, my hands were on his little head, praying in tongues for his destiny. One morning he came leaping on to the bus. He said, "Guess what? Last night I talked to God." This took me by surprise! "What did you say to God?" "I asked Him to help me be good for the rest of my life." "What did God say to you?" "He said he was going to help me."

"Did you ask Him to live in your heart?"

"Oh yes, but that was a couple of nights ago when the bright light came by my bed."

The next Sunday we were in church, Robert asked if we could hold hands and pray. I led him in a salvation prayer to seal his faith. Then I explained to him what communion was. Bill, Robert and I shared communion and then the Holy Spirit rested noticeably on Robert's little face. He said, "Rosey, I feel tingles on my hands and face. They feel hot."

"It's OK Robert," I said, "it's Jesus. That's the way He kisses His best friends." I wanted him to know that Jesus was his best friend for the rest of his life. In his circumstances, there were no guarantees he would be in this district for very long.

During this season, the rest of the students on my bus gave their lives to the Lord. Even my aide renewed her commitment to Christ. God's signature was all over these bus-driving jobs in spite of my desire to have a different job description. I felt strategically placed.

Sometimes I wondered just what would have happened if I didn't yield to the leading of the Lord. Where would I be? What would I be doing? Most of the time, God asks me to do things I don't have desire for. In the flesh yielding is not so easy, but it's always rewarding in the end. When Jesus said to the Father, "Not my will, but yours be done," He was going through the same thing on a much deeper level.

Every one of the transitions we went through was hard on the flesh. Yet they all had the fingerprints of God on them. In each place we lived and worked, I took my feet to the street in prayer and it produced lasting fruit.

That's what being in love is all about, letting the love you have for Jesus shine wherever you are, however He wants to use you. Praying on site where the needs are, taking them to Jesus no matter how big or small. That's what being a Christian is all about. There is a great scripture that says it better than I can:

> *"For we are His workmanship, created in Christ Jesus for good works, which God prepared before-hand, that we should walk in them."*
> *Ephesians 2:10*

In between my bus runs I often walked up and down rows of parked buses asking Jesus to bring the drivers to salvation and then use them to bring in the people of Grandview. Bill was praying daily for his boss' salvation. His prayers were answered fast. In less than three months, Charlie gave his life to Christ. He and his wife began attending a good Bible-believing church.

Charlie had lots of questions so their workday was filled with beautiful conversations about Jesus. It's important to clean the fish you catch. A fish left out of water will die and be of no value, but a filleted fish makes a good meal.

One afternoon Charlie said to me, "A brand new bus just arrived and you're going to be driving it."

"My months of employment don't qualify me to get a new bus," I said. "Several drivers have over 20 years of seniority. I don't need a big one, the one I have is fine."

"You get the bus and if you have any problems, you'll need to take it up with the Boss," Charlie replied.

I spoke with the supervisor and his reply was, "You are getting the new bus whether you like it or not. I think you're the one who will take the best care of it." I was stunned.

The number printed on the new bus was No.3 I took notice of the numbers to see if the Lord was saying anything. Three stands for what is solid, real and God's complete divine perfection. The trinity is an example of this.

A month later Charlie came out and painted over No.3 and changed it to No.2. This puzzled me. No.11 and No.3 seemed significant but I didn't have a clue what No.2 meant.

In a conversation with a friend, she mentioned that the number two denoted that the Lord would determine the matter. She understood this from the story of Joseph. Joseph told Pharaoh that God gave him two dreams and this meant that the Lord would determine the matter *(Genesis 41:32)*. There was a strong witness in my spirit for this interpretation; the problem was I didn't know what to do with it. One thing I knew in the natural though, the sparks were going to fly among the other drivers when I started driving this new bus. I decided to tell them it was an order from the boss and I had no choice. Visibility in this bus was tremendous. It was equipped with mirror defrosters, cruise control, tinted windows, and it sat up high. I had a grander view of everything, greater than any bus I had ever driven! All these conveniences made my job easier. God Himself was putting me in a new place that I didn't think I needed or wanted.

This seemed to parallel what was happening in our church. His higher ways and greater wisdom had to put us in this new spiritual vehicle whether we liked it or not. We needed this grander visibility if we wanted to do what the Lord was doing. We would miss His best if we stayed where we were. He wanted to promote us to a higher place, give us a grander view of the spiritual realm around us, but we had to take the new bus in spite of what others would think. Mercy was falling to give us what we needed even when we were perfectly content with what we had. In the world people are entitled to positions because of their seniority, but God's favor supersedes man's ways. His plan will violate all man's systems to bring forth His purposes. How thankful we should be that it's not about our race, gender, nor our years of service. It's all about Jesus and his unconditional love for us and His divine orders. He is the All-wise and All-knowing Judge and it's up to Him to determine the matter.

I was quite involved with the prayer meetings at our church. My pastor, Mike Bickle invited me to join a new team he developed called the PRAYER COUNCIL. I thought it was best to just sit back and watch how things operated. Much to my surprise, many of the things I had been involved with previously arose as suggestions. I was hesitant expressing an interest because I nailed everything to the cross in Texas. It was important for me to wait for the new thing God would show me in spite of my excitement to see these areas developed. I would faithfully wait for the new blueprints to unfold that were handed to me in the scroll during my encounter with God before I got here.(refer to Chapter 10) It wasn't easy.

The more we met, the more I heard the Lord speak to me about prayerwalking and spiritual mapping. I didn't tell anyone at first; after all, I was the new kid on the block. I was still waiting to see what the Lord was going to do with us. In my private time, the Holy Spirit drew me to the library to research some of the history of the city. It became obvious that God desired to reveal hidden roots holding back the move of the Holy Spirit. Were there great and mighty things we didn't know, concealed in Grandview's history that were instrumental and vital to unlocking revival?

One evening as the Lord and I conversed, I was prompted to mobilize people to take their feet to the street in prayer once again. I had hoped to have a different spiritual job description here, just as I had hoped in the natural to do something different then driving a school bus. Someone must be diligently praying and prayerwalking is some how a significant part of the answer to those prayers.

The Lord told me it would look like I was alone at the beginning of this endeavor, but that He would be with me and would faithfully bring help when it was time. At the very next prayer council meeting part of this word proved true. I mentioned prayerwalking and there were no other members interested. Normally, I would have shelved the idea until unity came, except that the Lord had told me I would pioneer this alone for a season. When I brought up the subject of prayerwalks, Mike was kind and told me to move ahead with what was on my heart. He wanted me to test the spirit and see if God was indeed putting His hand to this.

I approached a few of the departmental leaders to see if they would consider prayerwalking with their groups. Each leader seemed enthused by the idea. I thought they were saying "yes" to be nice to me but wouldn't follow through. I was wrong. Many of them picked dates to do a prayerwalk. Was this really happening?

Even before I was sure that this was what I wanted to do, I grabbed hold of the Lord's cloak and hung on with all my might. It may have looked like I was leading this endeavor, but I knew I was being led. All I could think was, "Could this be one of the ways God will prepare this city for revival?" Seeing the results that on-site prayer had before, you might wonder as to why I would even question it. One never knows how God will move.

The first prayerwalk was launched through Grace Training Center. Forty excited people showed up. Each person was given a prayerwalk guideline sheet and a survey to fill out. The survey would help me see the responses to the methods they used and would also give us a good spiritual overview of the city of Grandview.

The survey had a spot to jot down words of knowledge and any demonic activity. The forty were divided into groups of three with an assigned leader. Each group was given a two-mile mapped out area, which would take about an hour to prayerwalk. With 13 groups we could pray through 26 miles of streets. In addition the Lord's direction was for us to pray for revival around all seven of the Grandview school buildings.

Everyone was clearly instructed that if they encountered a demonic stronghold, there was no hurry to remove it right then. It was important that people weren't led into warfare they were unprepared for. There is an old saying, "Fools rush in where angels fear to tread," and some of what we would find probably had been there a long time. This had often proved true in my past. It is wise to think the matter through in prayer and discern just how to administer the council of God. Our prayerwalking focus was to survey the land and pray for revival.

When everyone returned, each group shared the experience they had. Sam Storms, president of the training center said his group walked around a school building and he could feel a strong evil presence. "It felt like Satan was right there," he said. They targeted that area with prayer. When they finished, they turned the corner of the school building only to find bold graffiti that said, SATAN WAS HERE. Experiencing God's direction so clearly was a tremendous encouragement to them. Each group testified to experiencing higher levels of discernment and a keener sense of what to pray for than they had before. It was a very good start.

The following testimony is a true story of what happened that morning with one of the small groups.

## Testimony:

Dale Hensley and his wife Anita have lived in Grandview 24 years. Since they had experience with prayerwalking, they each led a team. Dale hoped to get a route by city hall, the pornography shop or the business center. Instead, his team was given a route within blocks of his home. Part of the route included the elementary school his sons had attended, a portion of the lake trail where he and his wife often prayerwalked and the city park where he coached his son's soccer team. Dale's first thought was to trade this route since he and Anita had covered this area at least a dozen times, but he headed out on the route with his team, Tonya and Jimmy.

Tonya received revelation not more than 100 yards into the walk. She pointed in the direction of a public walking trail and explained that she saw *little girls in danger in a wooded area where children play.* After the group had walked quite a bit of their route they reached the opposite corner of the park. Dale's attention was drawn to a wooded ten-acre lot adjacent to the park and school. The city had purchased it one year ago. This was where he and his wife had prayed and walked a number of times. As the team prayed, Dale noticed something. In the middle of the wooded area, barely visible from the path, was an old fruit cellar. The team was unprepared for what they found. The entire outside of the fruit cellar was plastered with curses and warnings. There were smears of red paint or possibly blood on the door.

They prayed as they entered the cellar. The walls were covered with occult graffiti, pentagrams, curses, symbols, and in large letters the words SATAN LOVES YOU. This was within 200 yards of the park, the city pool and the elementary school. There were no fences or barriers to prevent entry. They pled the blood of Jesus over the ground and the enemy's work. They also observed a couple of open wells. A yellow strip of police tape that said "DO NOT CROSS" was their only barrier. They prayed for the children that would come into this area and for the works of darkness to be demolished.

Dale knew something else needed to be done and asked the Lord for wisdom. Dale asked my opinion. (God had spoken to him in the car but he did not share that with the group). I suggested that since it was city property, we should notify someone in authority with the city. This confirmed the direction Dale received to tell his neighbor, Jim, a city alderman.

As Dale drove home, Jim was outside working on his car. Dale took him to the site explaining enough of the story to attract the alderman's concern for children's safety and the city's liability. As Jim observed the symbols and curses, his face turned white. Dale quietly prayed for Jim's safety and protection as Jim entered the cellar. Jim said he would immediately call the park commissioner and take him to the site.

Others of us kept this issue in prayer. Less than three weeks later Dale received an excited phone call from Jim. The cellar had been demolished with wrecking balls and the 37 feet open wells were filled in. Praise the Lord, this job was done very quickly, thanks to directions from the Holy Spirit and Dale's prayerful obedience.

*A word from Dale:* "My wife and I still walk by the place where God did battle for our city and the children. There is no remnant of the cellar or its history. We rejoice that victory was won, but we are still amazed that the site slipped our attention. We wonder, where else there remains hidden enemy activity? We are thankful for the organized prayerwalking efforts that began in our church and the favor the Lord allowed us to have with city authorities. I am still astonished that He answered so quickly through on-site prayer. We will continue to prayerwalk. God has shown us that if we will continue to prayerwalk, He will heal our land."

In Christ,
Dale Hensley

Within the first nine weeks of our first prayerwalks, nine different MCF departments participated. We were able to cover almost every street in Grandview, asking God to revive His Word and bring forth a harvest of souls. I thought excitement would fizzle out after the initial thrust, but it didn't. Our church outreach ministries requested that I organize prayerwalks throughout Kansas City to cover the streets where they held their meetings. Jeff and Dominic, friends who drive school buses got permission to use a bus to take us to the sites. Several times throughout the summer, we all loaded into a big school bus and drove to various sites in the city, worshipping on the way. Testimonies are numerous of how God moved and produced lasting fruit.

As the weather got colder, I thought interest would drop off. Instead, requests to organize teams continued until November. Our church's school, asked me to organize an indoor prayerwalk throughout the entire facility. It was very fruitful.

Another idea caught my attention. Often as I drove I noticed highway signs that said something like "This highway was adopted by the XYZ group to keep it litter free." I thought how prayer could keep our neighborhoods clean from spiritual garbage. This did not seem to be the time of year to start anything new, but I put out a little bait to see if God was in this idea. I made a sign-up sheet and sat in the back of the church for a few weeks. Without giving any public announcement, 65 people made a commitment for what I termed the ADOPT YOUR STREET program. I was surprised. It is a commitment to prayerwalk your own street or neighborhood once a week for one year. Within a short season of time the number grew by hundreds. Seeing this response, I realized the Lord was directing me again.

# Chapter 12

# *Feet Play A Significant Part*

Throughout this book, I emphasize the importance of praying on-site where you want to see the Lord touch down. In my journey through life I have witnessed much fruit from persistent on-site prayer, in and outside the walls of the church. In Chapter Four I explained how we are the "hands and feet" of God in the earth and the importance of knowing who is living inside us. I have also come to realize that our feet play a significant part in bringing God's presence to a street, town or targeted area.

Anything we believe should have its base in the Word of God. Let's examine some applicable scriptures. The first time we ever see God walking with man is in the book of Genesis. God walked and talked with Adam. That blows my mind!

> *"And they heard the sound of the Lord God walking in the garden in the cool of the day, and the man and his wife hid themselves from the presence of the Lord among the trees in the garden."*
>
> *Genesis 3:8*

Where God walks, His presence emanates. God's presence brought conviction to Adam and Eve after they sinned. What I want us to see is that God's presence came as a result of Him walking and placing His feet in the garden. It seems as though feet play a significant part in bringing the presence of God to mankind. Take a little "walk" through your Bible sometime and study the scriptures that talk about feet. You will be surprised how many times the word "foot" and "feet" are mentioned. (I have listed scripture references at the end of this chapter for your study).

In *Genesis 13:17* God tells Abraham, *"arise, walk about the land through its length and breath; for I will give it to you."* For some reason God wanted Abraham to touch his feet on the land that He was about to give him. God tells Abraham, Moses and Joshua the same thing about walking the land and receiving it as an inheritance. They were given the actual geographic location as their possession. We will not necessarily receive the deed of ownership today when our feet touch down as it was with the Old Testament saints. However, these same instructions are being given to the church today as a rhema word. The "land" being the lost souls. We can walk around our cities and believe God for a harvest of souls as our inheritance.

Look further. As we read on in the word, God's presence remained among the Israelites but now was confined to the Ark of the Covenant. Throughout scripture, we notice that wherever the Ark goes, God's presence goes.

In *Joshua 3:13-17* we read,

> *"And it shall come about when the soles of the feet of the priest who carry the ark of the Lord, the Lord of all the earth, shall rest in the waters of the Jordan, that the waters of the Jordan shall be cut off and the waters which are flowing down from above shall stand in one heap."*

Why didn't God just tell them to throw the ark into the Jordan? I believe this was a prophetic action, prophesying the Father's desire for His presence to one day be living on the inside of us as a result of Christ's death, burial and resurrection.

God instructed them to carry the Ark into the water. He was basically saying, "let's do this together." It was the soles of their feet that touched down. God used their feet to release His power. As long as they were carrying the Ark, this miracle could occur.

130

As New Testament believers, this same presence lives within us! Wherever your feet go, 24 hours a day, the presence of God goes with you.

In both the Old and New Testament, the Lord references feet. *"...Heaven is my home and earth is my footstool"* *(Isaiah 66:1)*. Guess what? Now we have the Spirit of the Lord of all the earth, living inside of us. That means when our feet touch down, the presence of God touches down. The earth is His footstool through you. *"Do you not know this?"* Paul asked. *"Do you not know that you are the very sanctuary of the living God, His very temple?"*
        *1 Corinthians 6:19-20 emphasis added.*

In *2 Corinthians 6:17* it says, *"I will dwell in them and walk among them; I will be their God and they will be my people."* How is God going to walk among us? Is it possible that He is going to walk among us through our very own feet? I believe God wants to walk among His people in cooperation with them. If we consecrate ourselves and become more available to what He is doing, I think we'd be surprised as to how He would use us. I have gone through seasons where I was more sensitive to Him and dynamic things have happened.

God has a desire to walk among the lost. His will is that none of them should perish *(2 Peter 3:9)*. He loves them and wants to draw them into His embrace by working together in and through us. When you prayerwalk in your neighborhood, it's a prophetic drama of what God wants to do. He wants to shower them with His love. Once we realize the partnership offered, we can't help but cooperate with the Holy Spirit wherever we go. When we take our feet to the street, the laundromats and grocery stores in cooperation with Him, He touches down right there with us. The Lord of the universe is at the laundromat with you.

Look how *Exodus 24:9-10* describes what Moses, Aaron, Nadad, Abihu, and the 70 elders on the mountain are seeing, *"And they saw the God of Israel; and under His feet, there appeared to be a pavement of sapphire, as clear as the sky itself."* It fascinates me that the sapphire pavement was under God's feet.

In closing, I will share a visitation I had while writing this last chapter.

It was midnight on February 1, 1998. I was awakened by the Lord's presence. I remained in bed awake for a while basking under this anointing. Repeatedly *Song of Solomon 7:11* ran through my mind. I got up and read through to verse 13.

> *Come, my beloved, let us go out into the country, let us spend the night in the villages. Let us rise early and go to the vineyards; let us see whether the vine has budded and its blossoms have opened, and whether the pomegranates have bloomed. There I will give you my love. The mandrakes have given forth fragrance; and over our doors are all choice fruits, both new and old, which I have saved up for you, my beloved.*
>
> Song of Solomon 7:11-13

When I tried to return to my bed, I was gently pushed by an angel onto some pillows that were lying on the floor. At that moment, I realized the Lord wanted me to stay awake in His presence. As I yielded I felt a tremor in my spirit and scriptures concerning God's desire for the harvest flooded my mind. The following three scriptures came first:

> *"And after that He went out, and noticed a tax-gatherer named Levi, sitting in the tax office, and He said to him, 'Follow Me.' And he left everything behind, and rose and began to follow Him."*
>
> Luke 5:27-28

> *"So the woman left her waterpot, and went into the city, and said to the men, "Come, see a man who told me all the things that I have done; this is not the Christ, is it?" They went out of the city, and were coming to Him."*
>
> John 4:28-30

*Jesus said to them, "My food is to do the will of Him who sent Me, and to accomplish His work. "Do you not say, 'There are yet four months, and then comes the harvest'? Behold, I say to you, lift up your eyes, and look on the fields, that they are white for harvest. "Already he who reaps is receiving wages, and is gathering fruit for life eternal; that he who sows and he who reaps may rejoice together. "For in this case the saying is true, 'One sows, and another reaps.' "I sent you to reap that for which you have not labored; others have labored, and you have entered into their labor." And from that city many of the Samaritans believed in Him because of the word of the woman who testified, "He told me all the things that I have done."*

*John 4:34-39*

The inward audible voice of the Lord spoke to me, "Oh My beloved. How beautiful are the feet of him who brings good news. Your feet look so beautiful in sandals; in readiness, holiness, at peace with all men; shod with the preparation of the gospel; showing that your heart is ready to carry out My will. What faith you have to believe Me to touch the people outside the walls of the church."

I saw a vision of feet walking throughout the Kansas City streets crisscrossing one another and forming a big net. As they walked they crushed huge links of a chain, releasing freedom for the power of the gospel to go forth. They were literally shaking the gates of hell and setting captives free. The power of all the feet caused my body to shake. I heard the Lord continue, "Get ready and call forth the workers!" He assured me prayerwalking was not just another good idea. It is a part of His preparation for a mighty harvest.

*Luke 10:1-11* arose in my spirit,

*Now after this the Lord appointed seventy others, and sent them two and two ahead of Him to city and place where He Himself was going to come.*

133

> *And He was saying to them, "The harvest is plentiful, but the laborers are few; therefore beseech the Lord of the harvest to send out laborers into His harvest. Go your ways; behold, I send you out as lambs in the midst of wolves. Carry no purse, no bag, and no shoes; and greet no one on the way. And whatever house you enter, first say, 'Peace be to this house. And if a man of peace is there, your peace will rest upon him; but if not, it will return to you. And stay in that house, eating and drinking what they give you; for the laborer is worthy of his wages. Do not keep moving from house to house. And whatever city you enter, and they receive you, eat what is set before you; and heal those in it who are sick, and say to them, 'The kingdom of God has come near to you.' But whatever city you enter and they do not receive you, go out into its streets and say, 'Even the dust of your city which clings to our feet, we wipe off {in protest} against you; yet be sure of this, that the kingdom of God has come near.'*

The scroll mentioned in Chapter 10, which the Lord gave me in August of 1995, was now being opened up before me. In confirmation I opened my Bible to:

> *"And seeing the multitudes, He felt compassion for them, because they were distressed and downcast like sheep without a shepherd. Then He said to His disciples, "The harvest is plentiful, but the workers are few. "Therefore beseech the Lord of the harvest to send out workers into His harvest."*
>
> Matthew 9:36-38.

The Lord spoke to my spirit in this visitation. "I desire to spread my wings over the harvest and gather them under My shadow, the Shadow of the Almighty. I am giving you my method. Move and act."

I cried out, "But Lord this is too big for me!"

"It's for everyone," the Lord replied. "Station yourselves as watchmen in the gates of the city, on the highways and the by-ways, the fields are ripe and ready. Release the captives by speaking forth my Word. Then I will give the command for you to let down your nets for a big catch."

The Spirit of the Lord was showing me that when our prayers go outside the walls they create a big net that can contain a big catch. The Lord was crying out for Christians to be Christians wherever they are – praying, fasting, right on their own streets.

I heard voices all over the city calling out: "Make way! Make way for the King of Kings!" There were thousands of feet like a great army. The feet were crushing the chains, and the voices were proclaiming the Word of God over the city. The combination was leveling a path for the Lord to come and a voice shouted out, "It's like Joel's army ...nameless and faceless." Obedient Christians were on every street praying.

*Isaiah 61* rose up in my spirit, *"This is the favorable year of the Lord – Go forth and release the captives."* I couldn't count the feet and the catch wouldn't fit in any of our buildings.

A song flooded my head. It was one of the many songs imparted to me before we made our final decision to move here in 1995. This song had assured me God would visit Kansas City. These are the words:

> Look everyone, it's my lover.
> Listen to the sound, here he comes.
> He's leaping over the mountains
> and bounding over the hills.
> Look, He's gazing through the windows,
> peering through the lattice now.
> Saying 'arise my darling, my beautiful one.
> Arise my darling, come go with me.
> See the winter is past, the rains are over, and
> the flowers appear on the earth.
> The season has come for singing.
> Look everyone, it's King Jesus.
> Look everyone, it's your friend, your groom.
> Look up, everyone, it's your lover calling out to
> you. Come Go With Me!

All of a sudden I had an open vision of giant eyes looking in my windows from the outside. They were like God's eyes, filled with compassion and fire for His "LOST BRIDE" – the poor, the lonely, the lost, and the downtrodden.

"Go tell them Rosey, to look and listen. I am coming!"

He's coming to Kansas City.

I responded to the vision, there in my living room and began to shout to a multitude,

"Go out, Go outside the walls of the church!"

The Lord said, "I'm calling for you, and you're looking for Me, but you will not find Me until you come out into the streets. There I will give you my love."

Just before the Holy Spirit lifted His thick tangible presence, the following thoughts and Bible verses scrolled through my spirit. *Luke 17:24* and *Song of Solomon 7:1,* *"How beautiful are your footsteps,"* Verse 9, *"Your mouth is like the best of wine! Causing the lips of those who are asleep to speak."*

It is evident God wants to pour the best of wine out from the Bride's mouth. "Oh daughter, let your mouth drip with wine in the streets and call to whosoever will come to come." *Song of Solomon 7:11; (*See Also: *Luke 14:12-24; Luke 3:4-6; Isaiah 40; John 3:27-29; Matt 11:5-10).*

The visitation ended with;

> *"It's the year of Jubilee. Return to your own property (street) and eat the harvest."*
> *Leviticus 25:10-13*

It is certainly God's desire to make Kansas City His habitation. But not just Kansas City, your city too! Your feet play a significant part in preparing the way for His coming. Why not begin on your own street and start praying for the few neighbors that live next to you?

# *Epilogue*

God wants to use you as an instrument of revival to pray for your family, your friends and your city. Maybe you won't see instant results, but ask Him to give you tokens to keep you praying. God answers; He knows hope deferred makes the heart sick. He knows we need little victory tokens to keep us moving forward. In the natural, the gardener needs to see buds and blossoms to keep tending the garden. It is the same in the spiritual realm. God is desirous for you to enjoy your relationship together. Even when the ground of our hearts is hard, the Spirit shows Himself strong on our behalf by producing fruit for the kingdom and joy in your inner man.

As for me, I will continue to prayerwalk and seek the Lord for His divine guidance here in Grandview. My heart is crying out to our Heavenly Bridegroom to help us, His people, to take our *Feet to the Street* and prepare the way for His coming. I hope you have been encouraged to fall in love with Jesus and let Him be your best friend. Best friends like to be together all the time.

May those who are found faithful with a little, not only be given more, but also help to equip and mobilize others in the corporate life of their church. God will give us His grace to become His living messengers if we say "yes" to Him. So say Yes, and experience His divine entertainment wherever you go!

# *Appendix*

---

Listed below are just a few verses about feet:

*"Then He said, "Do not come near here; remove your sandals from your feet, for the place on which you are standing is holy ground."*

*Exodus 3:5*

*"except Caleb the son of Jephunneh; he shall see it, and to him and to his sons I will give the land on which he has set foot, because he has followed the Lord fully."*

*Deuteronomy 1:36*

*" '...Surely the land on which your foot has trodden shall be an inheritance to you and to your children forever, because you have followed the Lord my God fully.'"*

*Joshua 14:9*

*"And it shall be that when he lies down, that you shall notice the place where he lies and you shall go and uncover his feet and lie down; then he will tell you what you should do."*

*Ruth 3:4*

*"Now you arise, go to your house. When your feet enter the city the child will die."*

*1 Kings 14:12*

*"Then King David rose to his feet and said, 'Listen to me, my brethren and my people; I had intended to build a permanent home for the Ark*

of the Covenant of the Lord and for the footstool of our God. So I made preparations to build it.'"

*1 Chronicles 28:2*

"Thou dost make him to rule over the works of thy hands; Thou hast put all things under his feet."

*Psalms 8:6*

"He makes my feet like hinds' feet, and sets me upon high places."

*Psalms 18:33*

"He brought me up out of the pit of destruction, out of the miry clay; and set my feet upon a rock making my footsteps firm."

*Psalms 40:2*

"Thou shall tread upon the lion and the adder; the young lion and the dragon shall you trample under your feet" (KJV).

*Psalms 91:13*

"Thy Word is a lamp unto my feet, and a light to my path."

*Psalm 119:105*

"I dug wells and drank waters, and with the soles of my feet I dried up all the rivers of Egypt."

*Isaiah 37:25*

"How lovely on the mountains are the feet of him who brings good news, who announces peace and brings good news of happiness, who announces salvation, and says to Zion, 'Your God reigns!'"

*Isaiah 52:7*

*"The glory of Lebanon will come to you, The Juniper, the box tree, the Cypress together, to beautify the place of my sanctuary; and I shall make the place of my feet glorious."*

*Isaiah 60:13*

*"And he said to me, 'Son of man, this is the place of My throne and the place of the sole of my feet, where I will dwell among the sons of Israel forever....'"*

*Ezekiel 43:7*

*"Before him went the pestilence, and burning coals went forth at his feet" (KJV).*

*Habakkuk 3:5*

*"and ye shall tread down the wicked: for they shall be ashes under the soles of your feet in the day that I shall do this, saith the Lord of hosts" (KJV).*

*Malachi 4:3*

*"And whosoever shall not receive you, nor hear your words, when you depart out of that house or city, shake off the dust of your feet" (KJV).*

*Matthew 10:14*

*"And your feet shod with the preparation of the Gospel of peace; (KJV).*

*Ephesians 6:15*

*"And I saw a mighty Angel come down from heaven, clothed with a cloud: and a rainbow was upon his head, and his face was as it were the sun, and his feet as pillars of fire:" (KJV).*

*Revelation 10:1*